Dinosaurs

by William Diller Matthew

DINOSAURS.

TABLE OF CONTENTS.

Ankylosaurus.

CHAPTER IX.

The Beaked Dinosaurs (concluded). The Horned Dinosaurs--Triceratops, etc.

CHAPTER X.

Geographical Distribution of Dinosaurs.

CHAPTER XI.

Collecting Dinosaurs. How and Where they are Found. The First Discovery of Dinosaurs in the West. The Bone-Cabin Quarry. Fossil Hunting by Boat in Canada.

PREFACE.

This volume is in large part a reprint of various popular descriptions and notices in the American Museum Journal and elsewhere by Professor Henry Fairfield Osborn, Mr. Barnum Brown, and the writer. There has been a considerable demand for these articles which are now mostly out of print. In reprinting it seemed best to combine and supplement them so as to make a consecutive and intelligible account of the Dinosaur collections in the Museum. The original notices are quoted verbatim; for the remainder of the text the present writer is responsible. Professor S.W. Williston of Chicago University has kindly contributed a chapter--all too brief--describing the first discoveries of dinosaurs in the Western formations that have since yielded so large a harvest.

W. D. M.

CHAPTER I.

THE AGE OF REPTILES.

ITS ANTIQUITY, DURATION AND SIGNIFICANCE IN GEOLOGIC HISTORY.

Paleontology deals with the History of Life. Its time is measured in geologic epochs and periods, in millions of years instead of centuries. Man, by this measure, is but a creature of yesterday--his "forty centuries of civilization"[1] but a passing episode. It is by no means easy for us to adjust our perspective to the immensely long spaces of time involved in geological evolution. We are apt to think of all these extinct animals merely as prehistoric--to imagine them all living at the same time and contending with our cave-dwelling ancestors for the mastery of the earth.

In order to understand the place of the Dinosaurs in world-history, we must first get some idea of the length of geologic periods and the immense space of time separating one extinct fauna from another.

The Age of Man. Prehistoric time, as it is commonly understood, is the time when barbaric and savage tribes of men inhabited the world but before civilization began, and earlier than the written records on which history is based. This corresponds roughly to the Pleistocene epoch of geology; it is included along with the much shorter time during which civilization has existed, in the latest and shortest of the geological periods, the Quaternary. It was the age of the mammoth and the mastodon, the megatherium and Irish deer and of other quadrupeds large and small which are now extinct; but most of its animals were the same species as now exist. It was marked by the great episode of the Ice Age, when considerable parts of the earth's surface were buried under immense accumulations of ice, remnants of which are still with us in the icy covering of Greenland and Antarctica.

The Age of Mammals. Before this period was a very much longer one--at least thirty times as long--during which modern quadrupeds were slowly evolving from small and primitive ancestors into their present variety of form and size. This is the Tertiary Period or Age of Mammals. Through this long period we can trace step by step the successive stages through which the ancestors of horses, camels, elephants, rhinoceroses, etc., were gradually converted into their present form in adaptation to their various habits and environment. And with them were slowly evolved various kinds of quadrupeds whose descendants do not now exist, the Titanotheres, Elotheres, Oreodonts, etc., extinct races which have not survived to our time. Man, as such, had not yet come into existence, nor are we able to trace any direct and complete line of ancestry among the fossil species known to us; but his collateral ancestors were represented by the fossil species of monkeys and lemurs of the Tertiary period.

The Age of Reptiles. Preceding the Age of Mammals lies a long vista of geologic periods of which the later ones are marked by the dominance of Reptiles, and are grouped together as the Age of Reptiles or Mesozoic Era. This was the reign of the Dinosaurs, and in it we are introduced to a world of life so different from that of today that we might well imagine ourselves upon another planet.

None of the ordinary quadrupeds with which we are familiar then existed, nor any related to nor resembling them. But in their place were reptiles large and small, carnivorous and herbivorous, walking, swimming and even flying.

Crocodiles, Turtles and Sea Reptiles. The Crocodiles and Turtles of the swamps were not so very different from their modern descendants; there were also sea-crocodiles, sea-turtles, huge marine lizards (Mosasaurs) with flippers instead of feet; and another group of great marine reptiles (Plesiosaurs) somewhat like sea-turtles but with long neck and toothed jaws and without any carapace. These various kinds of sea-reptiles took the place of the great sea mammals of modern times (which were evolved during the Age of Mammals); of whales and dolphins, seals and walruses, and manatees.

Pterodactyls. The flying Reptiles or Pterosaurians, partly took the place of birds, and most of them were of small size. Strange bat-winged creatures, the wing membrane stretched on the enormously elongated fourth finger, they are of all extinct reptiles the least understood, the most difficult to reconstruct and visualize as they were in life.

Dinosaurs. The land reptiles were chiefly Dinosaurs, a group which flourished throughout the Age of Reptiles and became extinct at its close. "Dinosaur" is a general term which covers as wide a variety in size and appearance as "Quadruped" among modern animals. And the Dinosaurs in the Age of Reptiles occupied about the same place in nature as the larger quadrupeds do today. They have been called the Giant Reptiles, for those we know most about were gigantic in size, but there were also numerous smaller kinds, the smallest no larger than a cat. All of them had short, compact bodies, long tails, and long legs for a reptile, and instead of crawling, they walked or ran, sometimes upon all fours, more generally upon the hind limbs, like ostriches, the long tail balancing the weight of the body. Some modern lizards run this way on occasion, especially if they are in a hurry. But the bodies of lizards are too long and their limbs too small and slender for this to be the usual mode of progress, as it seems to have been among the Dinosaurs.

ANIMALS OF THE AGE OF REPTILES. LAND REPTILES. DINOSAURS corresponding to the larger quadrupeds or land mammals of today. CROCODILES, LIZARDS AND TURTLES still surviving. SEA REPTILES. PLESIOSAURS } corresponding to whales, dolphins, seals, ICHTHYOSAURS } etc., or sea-mammals of today. MOSASAURS } FLYING REPTILES OR PTEROSAURS. BIRDS WITH TEETH (scarce and little known). PRIMITIVE MAMMALS of minute size (scarce and little known). FISHES and INVERTEBRATES many of them of extinct races, all more or less different from modern kinds.

Fishes, large and small, were common in the seas and rivers of the Age of Reptiles but all of them were more or less different from modern kinds, and many belonged to ancient races now rare or extinct.

The lower animals or Invertebrates were also different from those of today, although some would not be very noticeably so at first glance. Among molluscs, the Ammonites, related to the modern Pearly Nautilus, are an example of a race very numerous and varied during all the periods of the Reptilian Era, but disappearing at its close, leaving only a few collateral descendants in the squids, cuttlefish and nautili of the modern seas. The Brachiopods were another group of molluscs, or rather molluscoids for they were not true molluscs, less abundant even then than in previous ages and now surviving only in a few rare and little known types such as the lamp-shell (Terebratulina).

Insects. The Insect life of the earlier part of the Age of Reptiles was notable for the absence of all the higher groups and orders, especially those adapted to feed on flowers. There were no butterflies or moths, no bees or wasps or ants although there were plenty of dragonflies, cockroaches, bugs and beetles. But in the latter part of this era, all these higher orders appeared along with the flowering plants and trees.

Plants. The vegetation in the early part of the era was very different both from the gloomy forests of the more ancient Coal Era and from that which prevails today. Cycads, ferns and fern-like plants, coniferous trees, especially related to the modern Araucaria or Norfolk Island Pine, Ginkgos still surviving in China, and huge equisetae or horsetail rushes, still surviving in South American swamps and with dwarfed relatives throughout the world, were the dominant plant types of that era. The flowering plants and deciduous trees had not appeared. But in the latter half of the era these appeared in ever increasing multitudes, displacing the lower types and relegating them to a subordinate position. Unlike the more rapidly changing higher animals these ancient Mesozoic groups of plants have not wholly disappeared, but still survive, mostly in tropical and southern regions or as a scanty remnant in contrast with their once varied and dominant role.

There is every reason to believe that upon the appearance of these higher plants whose flower and fruit afforded a more concentrated and nourishing food, depended largely the evolution of the higher animal life both vertebrate and insect, of the Cenozoic or modern era.

FOOTNOTES:

[Footnote 1: The records of Egypt and Chaldaea extend back at least sixty centuries.]

CHAPTER II.

NORTH AMERICA IN THE AGE OF REPTILES.

ITS GEOGRAPHIC AND CLIMATIC CHANGES.

North America in the Age of Reptiles would have seemed almost as strange to our eyes in its geography as in its animals and plants. The present outlines of its coast, its mountains and valleys, its rivers and lakes, have mostly arisen since that time. Even the more ancient parts of the continent have been profoundly modified through the incessant work of rain and rivers and of the waves, tending to wear down the land surfaces, of volcanic outbursts building them up, and of the more mysterious agencies which raise or depress vast stretches of mountain chains or even the whole area of a continent, and which tend on the whole so far as we can see, to restore or increase the relief of the continents, as the action of the surface waters tends to bring them down to or beneath the sea level.

Alternate Overflow and Emergence of Continents. In a broad way these agencies of elevation and of erosion have caused in their age-long struggle an alternation of periods of overflow and periods of continental emergence during geologic time. During the periods of overflow, great portions of the low-lying parts of the continents were submerged, and formed extensive but comparatively shallow seas. The mountains through long continued erosion were reduced to gentle and uniform slopes of comparatively slight elevation. Their materials were brought down by rivers to the sea-coast, and distributed as sedimentary formations over the shallow interior seas or along the margins of the continents. But this load of sediments, transferred from the dry land to the ocean margins and shallow seas, disturbed the balance of weight (isostasy) which normally keeps the continental platforms above the level of the ocean basins (which as shown by gravity measurement are underlain by materials of higher specific gravity than the continents). In due course of time, when the strain became sufficient, it was readjusted by earth movements of a slowness proportioned to their vastness. These movements while tending upon the whole to raise the continents to or sometimes beyond their former relief, did not reverse the action of erosion agencies in detail, but often produced new lines or areas of high elevation.

Geologic Periods. A geologic period is the record of one of these immense and long continued movements of alternate submergence and elevation of the continents. It begins, therefore, and ends with a time of emergence, and includes a long era of submergence.

These epochs of elevation are accompanied by the development of cold climates at the poles, and elsewhere of arid conditions in the interior of the continents. The epochs of submergence are accompanied by a warm, humid climate, more or less uniform from the equator to the poles.

The earth has very recently, in a geologic sense, passed through an epoch of extreme continental elevation the maximum of which was marked by the "Ice Age." The continents are still emerged for the most part almost to the borders of the "continental shelf" which forms their maximum limit. And in the icy covering of Greenland and Antarctica a considerable portion still remains of the great ice-sheets which at their maximum covered large parts of North America and Europe. We are now at the beginning of a long period of slow erosion and subsidence which, if this interpretation of the geologic record be correct, will in the course of time reduce the mountains to plains and submerge great parts of the lowlands beneath the ocean. As compensation for the lesser extent of dry land we may look forward to a more genial and favorable climate in the reduced areas that remain above water.

Length of Geologic Cycles. But these vast cycles of geographic and climatic change will take millions of years to accomplish their course. The brief span of human life, or even the few centuries of recorded civilization are far too short to show any perceptible change in climate due to this cause. The utmost stretch of a man's life will cover perhaps one-two hundred thousandth part of a geologic period. The time elapsed since the dawn of civilization is less than a three-thousandth part. Of the days and hours of this geologic year, our historic records cover but two or three minutes, our individual lives but a fraction of a second. We must not expect to find records of its changing seasons in human history, still less to observe them personally.

There are indeed minor cycles of climate within this great cycle. The great Ice Age through which the earth has so recently passed was marked by alternations of severity and mildness of climate, of advance and recession of the glaciers, and within these smaller cycles are minor alternations whose effect upon the course of human history has been shown recently by Professor Huntington ("The Pulse of Asia"). But the great cycles of the geologic periods are of a scope far too vast for their changes to be perceptible to us except through their influence upon the course of evolution.

The Later Cycles of Geologic Time. The Reptilian Era opens with a period of extreme elevation, which rivalled that of the Glacial Epoch and was similarly accompanied by extensive glaciation of which some traces are preserved to our day in characteristic glacial boulders, ice scratches, and till, imbedded or inter-stratified in the strata of the Permian age. Between these two extremes of continental emergence, the Permian and the Pleistocene, we can trace six cycles of alternate submergence and elevation, as shown in the diagram (Fig. 5), representing the proportion of North America which is known to have been above water during the six geologic periods that intervene.

From this diagram it will appear that the six cycles or periods were by no means equal in the amount of overflow or complete recovery of the drowned lands. The Cretacic period was marked by a much more extensive and long continued flooding; the great plains west of the Mississippi were mostly under water from the Gulf of Mexico to the Arctic Ocean. The earlier overflows were neither so extensive nor so long continued. The great uplift of the close of the Cretacic regained permanently the great central region and united East and West, and the overflows of the Age of Mammals were mostly limited to the South Atlantic and Gulf coasts.

Sedimentary Formations. During the epochs of greatest overflow great marine formations were deposited over large areas of what is now dry land. These were followed as the land rose to sea level by extensive marsh and delta formations, and these in turn by scattered and fragmentary dry land deposits spread by rivers over their flood plains. In the marine formations are found the fossil remains of the sea-animals of the period; in the coast and delta formations are the remains of those which inhabited the marshes and forests of the coast regions; while the animals of the dryland, of plains and upland, left their remains in the river-plain formations.

These last, however, fragmentary and loose and overlying the rest, were the first to be swept away by erosion during the periods of elevation; and of such formations in the Age of Reptiles very little, if anything, seems to have been preserved to our day. Consequently we know very little about the upland animals of those times, if as seems very probable, they were more or less different from the animals of the coast-forests and swamps. The river-plain deposits of the Age of Mammals on the other hand, are still quite extensive, especially those of its later epochs, and afford a fairly complete record in some parts of the continent of the upland fauna of those regions.

Occurrence of Dinosaur Bones. Dinosaur bones are found mostly in the great delta formations, and since those were accumulated chiefly in the early stages of great continental elevations, it follows that our acquaintance with Dinosaurs is mostly limited to those living at certain epochs during the Age of Reptiles. In point of fact so far as explorations have yet gone in this country, the Dinosaur fauna of the close of the Jurassic and beginning of the Comanchic and that of the later Cretacic are the only ones we know much about. The immense interval of time that preceded, and the no less vast stretch of time that separated them, is represented in the record of Dinosaur history by a multitude of tracks and a few imperfect skeletons assigned to the close of the Triassic period, and by a few fragments from formations which may be intermediate in age between the Jurassic-Comanchic and the late Cretacic. Consequently we cannot expect to trace among the Dinosaurs, the gradual evolution of different races, as we can do among the quadrupeds of the Age of Mammals.

Imperfection of the Geologic Record. The Age of Mammals in North America presents a moving picture of the successive stages in the evolution of modern quadrupeds; the Age of Reptiles shows (broadly considered) two photographs representing the land vertebrates of two long distant periods, as remote in time from each other as the later one is remote from the present day. Of the earlier stages in the evolution of the Dinosaurs there are but a few imperfect sketches in this country; in Europe the picture is more complete. In the course of time, as exploration progresses, we shall no doubt recover more complete records. But probably we shall never have so complete a history of the terrestrial life of the Age of Reptiles as we have of the Age of Mammals. The records are defective, a large part of them destroyed or forever inaccessible.

CHAPTER III.

KINDS OF DINOSAURS.

COMMON CHARACTERS AND DIFFERENCES BETWEEN THE VARIOUS GROUPS.

In the preceding chapter we have attempted to point out the place in nature that the Dinosaurs occupied and the conditions under which they lived. They were the dominant land animals of their time, just as the quadrupeds were during the Age of Mammals. Their sway endured for a long era, estimated at nine millions of years, and about three times as long as the period which has elapsed since their disappearance. They survived vast changes in geography and climate, and became extinct through a combination of causes not fully understood as yet; probably the great changes in physical conditions at the end of the Cretacic period, and the development of mammals and birds, more intelligent, more active, and better adapted to the new conditions of life, were the most important factors in their extinction.

The Dinosaurs originated, so far as we can judge, as lizard-like reptiles with comparatively long limbs, long tails, five toes on each foot, tipped with sharp claws, and with a complete series of sharp pointed teeth. It would seem probable that these ancestors were more or less bipedal, and adapted to live on dry land. They were probably much like the modern lizards in size, appearance and habitat:[2]

From this ancestral type the Dinosaurs evolved into a great variety of different kinds, many of them of gigantic size, some herbivorous, some carnivorous; some bipedal, others quadrupedal; many of them protected by various kinds of bony armor-plates, or provided with horns or spines; some with sharp claws, others with blunted claws or hoofs.

These various kinds of Dinosaurs are customarily grouped as follows:

I. Carnivorous Dinosaurs or Theropoda. With sharp pointed teeth, sharp claws; bipedal, with bird-like hind feet, generally three-toed;[3] the fore-limbs adapted for grasping or tearing, but not for support of the body. The head is large, neck of moderate length, body unarmored. The principal Dinosaurs of this group in America are

Allosaurus, Ornitholestes--Upper Jurassic period.

Tyrannosaurus, Deinodon, Albertosaurus, Ornithomimus--Upper Cretacic period.

II. Amphibious Dinosaurs or Sauropoda. With blunt-pointed teeth and blunt claws, quadrupedal, with elephant-like limbs and feet, long neck and small head. Unarmored. Principal dinosaurs of this group in America are Brontosaurus, Diplodocus, Camarasaurus (Morosaurus) and Brachiosaurus, all of the Upper Jurassic and Comanchic periods.

III. Beaked Dinosaurs or Predentates. With a horny beak on the front of the jaw, cutting or grinding teeth behind it. All herbivorous, with pelvis of peculiar type, with hoofs instead of claws, and many genera heavily armored. Mostly three short toes on the hind foot, four or five on the fore foot. This group comprises animals of very different proportions as follows:

1. Iguanodonts. Bipedal, unarmored, with a single row of serrated cutting teeth, three-toed hind feet. Upper Jurassic, Comanchic and Cretacic. Camptosaurus is the best known American genus.

2. Trachodonts or Duck-billed Dinosaurs. Like the Iguanodonts but with numerous rows of small teeth set close together to form a grinding surface. Cretacic period. Trachodon, Hadrosaurus, Claosaurus, Saurolophus, Corythosaurus, etc.

3. Stegosaurs or Armored Dinosaurs. Quadrupedal dinosaurs with elephantine feet, short neck, small head, body and tail armored with massive bony plates and often with large bony spines. Teeth in a single row, like those of Iguanodonts. Stegosaurus of the Upper Jurassic, Ankylosaurus of the Upper Cretacic.

4. Ceratopsian or Horned Dinosaurs. Quadrupedal with elephantine feet, short neck, very large head enlarged by an enormous bony frill covering the neck, with a pair of horns over the eyes and a single horn in front. Teeth in a single row, but broadened out and adapted for grinding the food. No body armor. Triceratops is the best known type. Monoclonius, Ceratops, Torosaurus and Anchiceratops are also of this group. All from the Cretacic period.

Classification of Dinosaurs. It is probable that the Dinosaurs are not really a natural group or order of reptiles, although they have been generally so considered. The Carnivorous and Amphibious Dinosaurs in spite of their diverse appearance and habits, are rather nearly related, while the Beaked Dinosaurs form a group apart, and may be descendants of a different group of primitive reptiles. These relations are most clearly seen in the construction of the pelvis (see fig. 9). In the first two groups the pubis projects downward and forward as it does in the majority of reptiles, and the ilium is a high rounded plate; while in the others the pelvis is of a wholly different type, strongly suggesting the pelvis of birds.

Recent researches upon Triassic dinosaurs, especially by the distinguished German savants, Friedrich von Huene, Otto Jaekel and the late Eberhard Fraas, and the discovery of more complete specimens of these animals, also clear up the true relationships of these primitive dinosaurs which have mostly been referred hitherto to the Theropoda or Megalosaurians. The following classification is somewhat more conservative than the arrangement recently proposed by von Huene.

ORDER SAURISCHIA Seeley. Suborder Coelurosauria von Huene (=Compsognatha Huxley, Symphypoda Cope.) Fam. Podokesaurid?Triassic, Connecticut. " Hallopodid?Jurassic, Colorado. " Coelurid?Jurassic and Comanchic, North America. " Compsognathid?Jurassic, Europe. Suborder Pachypodosauria von Huene. Fam. Anchisaurid?Triassic, North America and Europe. " Zanclodontid?} " Plateosaurid?} Triassic, Europe.* Suborder Theropoda Marsh (=Goniopoda Cope) Fam. Megalosaurid?Jurassic and Comanchic. " Deinodontid?Cretacic. " Ornithomimid?Cretacic, North America. Suborder Sauropoda Marsh (=Opisthocoelia Owen, Cetiosauria Seeley.) Fam. Cetiosaurid?} " Morosaurid?} Jurassic and Comanchic. " Diplodocid?} Order ORNITHISCHIA Seeley (=Orthopoda Cope, Predentata Marsh.) Suborder Ornithopoda Marsh (Iguanodontia Dollo) Fam. Nanosaurid?Jurassic, Colorado. " Camptosaurid?} " Iguanodontid?} Jurassic and Comanchic. " Trachodontid?(=Hadrosaurid?, Cretacic. Suborder Stegosauria Marsh. Fam. Scelidosaurid?} Jurassic and Comanchic. " Stegosaurid?} " Ankylosaurid?(=Nodosaurid?, Cretacic. Suborder Ceratopsia Marsh. Fam. Ceratopsid?Cretacic.

* Regarded by Dr. von Huene as ancestral respectively to the Theropoda and Sauropoda.

FOOTNOTES:

[Footnote 2: If some vast catastrophe should today blot out all the mammalian races including man, and the birds, but leave the lizards and other reptiles still surviving, with the lower animals and plants, we might well expect the lizards in the course of geologic periods to evolve into a great and varied land fauna like the Dinosaurs of the Mesozoic Era.]

[Footnote 3: The ancestral types have four complete toes, but in the true Theropoda the inner digit is reduced to a small incomplete remnant, its claw reversed and projecting at the back of the foot, as in birds.]

CHAPTER IV.

THE CARNIVOROUS DINOSAURS, ALLOSAURUS, TYRANNOSAURUS, ORNITHOLESTES, ETC.

SUB-ORDER THEROPODA.

The sharp teeth, compressed and serrated like a palaeolithic spear point, and the powerful sharp-pointed curved claws on the feet, prove the carnivorous habits of these dinosaurs. The well-finished joints, dense texture of the hollow bones and strongly marked muscle-scars indicate that they were active and powerful beasts of prey. They range from small slender animals up to the gigantic Tyrannosaurus equalling the modern elephant in bulk. They were half lizard, half bird in proportions, combining the head, the short neck and small fore limbs and long snaky tail of the lizard with the short, compact body, long powerful hind limbs and three-toed feet of the bird. The skin was probably either naked or covered with horny scales as in lizards and snakes; at all events it was not armor-plated as in the crocodile.[4] They walked or ran upon the hind legs; in many of them the fore limbs are quite unfitted for support of the body and must have been used solely in fighting or tearing their prey.

The huge size of some of these Mesozoic beasts of prey finds no parallel among their modern analogues. It is only among marine animals that we find predaceous types of such gigantic size. But among the carnivorous dinosaurs we fail to find any indications of aquatic or even amphibious habits. They might indeed wade in the water, but they could hardly be at home in it, for they were clearly not good swimmers. We must suppose that they were dry land animals or at most swamp dwellers.

Dinosaur Footprints. The ancestors of the Theropoda appear first in the Triassic period, already of large size, but less completely bipedal than their successors. Incomplete skeletons have been found in the Triassic formations of Germany[5] but in this country they are chiefly known from the famous fossil footprints (or "bird-tracks" as they were at first thought to be), found in the flagstone quarries at Turner's Falls on the Connecticut River, in the vicinity of Boonton, New Jersey, and elsewhere. These tracks are the footprints of numerous kinds of dinosaurs, large and small, mostly of the carnivorous group, which lived in that region in the earlier part of the Age of Reptiles, and much has been learned from them as to the habits of the animals that made them. The tracks ascribed to carnivorous dinosaurs run in series with narrow tread, short or long steps, here and there a light impression of tail or forefoot and occasionally the mark of the shank and pelvis when the animal settled back and squatted down to rest a moment. The modern crocodiles when they lift the body off the ground, waddle forward with the short limbs wide apart, and even the lizards which run on their hind legs have a rather wide tread. But these dinosaurs ran like birds, setting one foot nearly in front of the other, so that the prints of right and left feet are nearly in a straight line. This was on account of their greater length of limb, which made it easy for them to swing the foot directly underneath the body at each step like mammals and birds, and thus maintain an even balance, instead of wabbling from side to side as short legged animals are compelled to do.

Of the animals that made these innumerable tracks the actual remains found thus far in this country are exceedingly scanty. Two or three incomplete skeletons of small kinds are in the Yale Museum, of which Anchisaurus is the best known.

Megalosaurus. Fragmentary remains of this huge carnivorous dinosaur were found in England nearly a century ago, and the descriptions by Dean Buckland and Sir Richard Owen and the restorations due to the imaginative chisel of Waterhouse Hawkins, have made it familiar to most English readers. Unfortunately it was, and still remains, very imperfectly known. It was very closely related to the American Allosaurus and unquestionably similar in appearance and habits.[6]

ALLOSAURUS.

The following extract is from the American Museum Journal for January 1908.[7]

"Although smaller than its huge contemporary Brontosaurus, this animal is of gigantic proportions being 34 feet 2 inches in length, and 8 feet 3 inches high."

History of the Allosaurus Skeleton. "This rare and finely preserved skeleton was collected by Mr. F.F. Hubbell in October 1879, in the Como Bluffs near Medicine Bow, Wyoming, the richest locality in America for dinosaur skeletons, and is a part of the great collection of fossil reptiles, amphibians and fishes gathered together by the late Professor E.D. Cope, and presented to the American Museum in 1899 by President Jesup.

"Shortly after the Centennial Exposition (1876) it had been planned that Professor Cope's collection of fossils should form part of a great public museum in Fairmount Park, Philadelphia, the city undertaking the cost of preparing and exhibiting the specimens, an arrangement similar to that existing between the American Museum and the City of New York.[8]

"The plan, however, fell through, and the greater part of this magnificent collection remained in storage in the basement of Memorial Hall in Fairmount Park, for the next twenty years. From time to time Professor Cope removed parts of the collection to his private museum in Pine Street, for purposes of study and scientific description. He seems, however, to have had no idea of the perfection and value of this specimen. In 1899 when the collection was purchased from his executors by Mr. Jesup, the writer went to Philadelphia under the instructions of Professor Osborn, Curator of Fossil Vertebrates, to superintend the packing and removal to the American Museum. At that time the collection made by Hubbell was still in Memorial Hall, and the boxes were piled up just as they came in from the West, never having been unpacked. Professor Cope's assistant, Mr. Geismar, informed the writer that Hubbell's collection was mostly fragmentary and not of any great value. Mr. Hubbell's letters from the field unfortunately were not preserved, but it is likely that they did not make clear what a splendid find he had made, and as some of his earlier collections had been fragmentary and of no great interest, the rest were supposed to be of the same kind.

"When the Cope Collection was unpacked at the American Museum, this lot of boxes, not thought likely to be of much interest, was left until the last, and not taken in hand until 1902 or 1903. But when this specimen was laid out, it appeared that a treasure had come to light. Although collected by the crude methods of early days, it consisted of the greater part of the skeleton of a single individual, with the bones in wonderfully fine preservation, considering that they had been buried for say eight million years. They were dense black, hard and uncrushed, even better preserved and somewhat more complete than the two fine skeletons of Allosaurus from Bone-Cabin Quarry, the greatest treasures that this famous quarry had supplied. The great carnivorous dinosaurs are much rarer than the herbivorous kinds, and these three skeletons are the most complete that have ever been found. In all the years of energetic exploration that the late Professor Marsh devoted to searching for dinosaurs in the Jurassic and Cretaceous formations of the West, he did not obtain any skeletons of carnivorous kinds anywhere near as complete as these, and their anatomy was in many respects unknown or conjectural. By comparison of the three Allosaurus skeletons with one another and with other specimens of carnivorous dinosaurs of smaller size in this and other museums, particularly in the National Museum and the Kansas University Museum, we have been able to reconstruct the missing parts of the Cope specimen with very little possibility of serious error."

Evidence for Combining and Posing this Mount. "An incomplete specimen of Brontosaurus, found by Doctor Wortman and Professor W.C. Knight of the American Museum Expedition of 1897, had furnished interesting data as to the food and habits of Allosaurus, which were confirmed by several other fragmentary specimens obtained later in the Bone-Cabin Quarry. In this Brontosaurus skeleton several of the bones, especially the spines of the tail vertebrae, when found in the rock, looked as if they had been scored and bitten off, as though by some carnivorous animal which had either attacked the Brontosaurus when alive, or had feasted upon the carcass. When the Allosaurus jaw was compared with these score marks, it was found to fit them exactly, the spacing of the scratches being the same as the spacing of the teeth. Moreover, on taking out the Brontosaurus vertebrae from the quarry, a number of broken off teeth of Allosaurus were found lying beside them. As no other remains of Allosaurus or any other animal were intermingled with the Brontosaurus skeleton, the most obvious explanation was that these teeth were broken off by an Allosaurus while devouring the Brontosaurus carcass. Many of the bones of other herbivorous dinosaurs found in the Bone-Cabin Quarry were similarly scored and bitten off, and the teeth of Allosaurus were also found close to them.

"With these data at hand the original idea was conceived of combining these two skeletons, both from the same formation and found within a few miles of each other, to represent what must actually have happened to them in the remote Jurassic period, and mount the Allosaurus skeleton standing over the remains of a Brontosaurus in the attitude of feeding upon its carcass. Some modifications were made in the position to suit the exigencies of an open mount, and to accommodate the pose to the particular action; the head of the animal was lifted a little, one hind foot planted upon the carcass, while the other, resting upon the ground bears most of the weight. The fore feet, used in these animals only for fighting or for tearing their prey, not for support, are given characteristic attitudes, and the whole pose represents the Allosaurus devouring the carcass and raising head and fore foot in a threatening manner as though to drive away intruders. The balance of the various parts was carefully studied and adjusted under direction of the curator. The preparation and mounting of the specimen were done by Mr. Adam Hermann, head preparator, and his assistants, especially Messrs. Falkenbach and Lang.

"As now exhibited in the Dinosaur Hall, this group gives to the imaginative observer a most vivid picture of a characteristic scene in that bygone age, millions of years ago, when reptiles were the lords of creation, and 'Nature, red in tooth and claw' had lost none of her primitive savagery, and the era of brute force and ferocity showed little sign of the gradual amelioration which was to come to pass in future ages through the predominance of superior intelligence."

Appearance and Habits of Allosaurus. A study of the mechanism of the Allosaurus skeleton shows us in the first place that the animal is balanced on the hind limbs, the long heavy tail making an adequate counterpoise for the short compact body and head. The hind limbs are nine feet in length when extended, about equal to the length of the body and neck, and the bones are massively proportioned. When the thigh bone is set in its normal position, as indicated by the position of the scars and processes for attachment of the principal muscles (see under Brontosaurus for the method used to determine this), the knee bends forward as in mammals and birds, not outward as in most modern reptiles. The articulations of the foot bones show that the animal rested upon the ends of the metapodials, as birds and many mammals do, not upon the sole of the foot like crocodiles or lizards. The flat vertebral joints show that the short compact body was not as flexible as the longer body of crocodiles or lizards, in which the articulations are of the ball and socket type showing that in them this region was very flexible. The tail also shows a limited flexibility. It could not be curled or thrown over the back, but projected out behind the animal, swinging from side to side or up and down as much as was needed for balance. The curvature of the ribs shows that the body was narrow and deep, unlike the broad flattened body of the crocodile or the less flattened but still broad body of the lizard. The loose hung jaw, articulated far back, shows by the set of its muscles that it was capable of an enormous gape; while in the skull there is evidence of a limited movement of the upper jaw on the cranial portion, intended probably to assist in the swallowing of large objects, like the double jointed jaw of a snake.

As to the nature of the skin we have no exact knowledge. We may be sure that it had no bony armor like the crocodile, for remains of any such armor could not fail to be preserved with the skeletons, as it always is in fossil crocodiles or turtles. Perhaps it was scaly like the skin of lizards and snakes, for the horny scales of the body are not preserved in fossil skeletons of these reptiles. But if so we might expect from the analogy of the lizard that the scales of the head would be ossified and preserved in the fossil; and there is nothing of this kind in the Carnivorous Dinosaurs. We can exclude feathers from consideration, for these dinosaurs have no affinities to birds, and there is no evidence for feathers in any dinosaur. Probably the best evidence is that of the Trachodon or duck-billed dinosaur although this animal was but distantly related to the Allosaurus. In Trachodon (see p. 94), we know that the skin bore neither feathers nor overlapping scales but had a curiously patterned mosaic of tiny polygonal plates and was thin and quite flexible. Some such type of skin as this, in default of better evidence, we may ascribe to the Allosaurus.

As to its probable habits, it is safe to infer (see p. 33), that it was predaceous, active and powerful, and adapted to terrestrial life. Its methods of attack and combat must have been more like those of modern reptiles than the more intelligent methods of the mammalian carnivore. The brain cast of Allosaurus indicates a brain of similar type and somewhat inferior grade to that of the modern crocodile or lizard, and far below the bird or mammal in intelligence. The keen sense of smell of the mammal, the keen vision of the bird, the highly developed reasoning power of both, were absent in the dinosaur as in the lizard or crocodile. We may imagine the Allosaurus lying in wait, watching his prey until its near approach stimulates him into a semi-instinctive activity; then a sudden swift rush, a fierce snap of the huge jaws and a savage attack with teeth and claws until the victim is torn in pieces or swallowed whole. But the stealthy, persistent tracking of the cat or weasel tribe, the intelligent generalship of the wolf pack, the well planned attack at the most vulnerable point in the prey, characteristic of all the predaceous mammals, would be quite impossible to the dinosaur. By watching the habits of modern reptiles we may gain a much better idea of his capacities and limitations than if we judge only from the efficiency of his teeth and claws, and forget the inferior intelligence that animated these terrible weapons.

TYRANNOSAURUS.

The "Tyrant Saurian" as Professor Osborn has named him, was the climax of evolution of the giant flesh-eating dinosaurs. It reached a length of forty-seven feet, and in bulk must have equalled the mammoth or the mastodon or the largest living elephants. The massive hind limbs, supporting the whole weight of the body, exceeded the limbs of the great proboscideans in bulk, and in a standing position the animal was eighteen to twenty feet high, as against twelve for the largest African elephants or the southern mammoth. The head (see frontispiece) is 4 feet 3 inches long, 3 ft. 4 inches deep, and 2 ft. 9 inches wide; the long deep powerful jaws set with teeth from 3 to 6 inches long and an inch wide. To this powerful armament was added the great sharp claws of the hind feet, and probably the fore feet, curved like those of eagles, but six or eight inches in length.

During ten years explorations in the Western Cretaceous formations, Mr. Brown has secured for the Museum three skeletons of this magnificent dinosaur, incomplete, but finely preserved. The first, found in 1900, included the jaws, a large part of backbone and ribs, and some limb bones. The second included most of skull and jaws, backbone, ribs and pelvis and the hind limbs and feet, but not tail. The third consisted of a perfect skull and jaws, the backbone, ribs, pelvis and nearly all of the tail, but no limbs. From these three specimens it has been possible to reconstruct the entire skeleton. The exact construction of the fore feet is the only doubtful part. The fore-limb is very small relatively to the huge size of the animal, but probably was constructed much as in the Allosaurus with two or three large curved claws, the inner claw opposing the others.

The missing parts of the two best skeletons have been restored, and with the help of two small models of the skeleton, a group has been made ready for mounting as the central piece of the proposed Cretaceous Dinosaur Hall. One of the skeletons is temporarily placed in the centre of the Quaternary Hall, space for it in the present Dinosaur Hall being lacking. Following is Professor Osborn's description of the preparation of this group:[9]

"The mounting of these two skeletons presents mechanical problems of very great difficulty. The size and weight of the various parts are enormous. The height of the head in the standing position reaches from 18 to 20 feet above the ground; the knee joint alone reaches 6 feet above the ground. All the bones are massive; the pelvis, femur and skull are extremely heavy. Experience with Brontosaurus and with other large dinosaurs proves that it is impossible to design a metallic frame in the right pose in advance of assembling the parts. Even a scale restoration model of the animal as a whole does not obviate the difficulty.

"Accordingly in preparing to mount Tyrannosaurus for exhibition a new method has been adopted, namely, to prepare a scale model of every bone in the skeleton and mount this small skeleton with flexible joints and parts so that all studies and experiments as to pose can be made with the models.

"This difficult and delicate undertaking was entrusted to Mr. Erwin Christman of the artistic staff of the Department of Vertebrate Palaeontology of the Museum, who has prepared two very exact models to a one-sixth scale, representing our two skeletons of Tyrannosaurus rex, which fortunately are of exactly the same size. A series of three experiments by Mr. Christman on the pose of Tyrannosaurus, under the direction of the author and Curator Matthew, were not satisfactory. The advice of Mr. Raymond L. Ditmars, Curator of Reptiles in the New York Zoological Park, was sought and we thus obtained the fourth pose, which is shown in the photographs published herewith.

"The fourth pose or study, for the proposed full sized mount, is that of two reptiles of the same size attracted to the same prey. One reptile is crouching over its prey (which is represented by a portion of a skeleton). The object of this depressed pose is to bring the perfectly preserved skull and pelvis very near the ground within easy reach of the visiting observer. The second reptile is advancing, and attains very nearly the full height of the animal. The general effect of this group is the best that can be had and is very realistic, particularly the crouching figure. A fifth study will embody some further changes. The upright figure is not well balanced and will be more effective with the feet closer together, the legs straighter and the body more erect. These reptiles have a series of strong abdominal ribs not shown in the models. The fourth position places the pelvis in an almost impossible position as will be noted from the ischium and pubis.

"The lateral view of this fourth pose represents the animals just prior to the convulsive single spring and tooth grip which distinguishes the combat of reptiles from that of all mammals, according to Mr. Ditmars.

"The rear view of the standing skeleton displays the peculiarly avian structure of the iliac junction with the sacral plate, characteristic of these very highly specialized dinosaurs, also the marked reduction of the upper end of the median metatarsal bone, which formerly was believed to be peculiar to Ornithomimus."

This model of the group is on exhibition with the mounted skeleton.

As compared with its predecessor Allosaurus, the Tyrannosaurus is much more massively proportioned throughout. The skull is more solid, the jaws much deeper and more powerful, the fore limb much smaller, the tail shorter, the hind limb straighter and the foot bones more compacted so that the animal was more strictly "digitigrade," approaching the ostriches more closely in this particular.

This animal probably reached the maximum of size and of development of teeth and claws of which its type of animal mechanism was capable. Its bulk precluded quickness and agility. It must have been designed to attack and prey upon the ponderous and slow moving Horned and Armored Dinosaurs with which its remains are found, and whose massive cuirass and weapons of defense are well matched with its teeth and claws. The momentum of its huge body involved a seemingly slow and lumbering action, an inertia of its movements, difficult to start and difficult to shift or to stop. Such movements are widely different from the agile swiftness which we naturally associate with a beast of prey. But an animal which exceeds an average elephant in bulk, no matter what its habits, is compelled by the laws of mechanics to the ponderous movements appropriate to its gigantic size. These movements, directed and controlled by a reptilian brain, must needs be largely automatic and instinctive. We cannot doubt indeed that the Carnivorous Dinosaurs developed, along with their elaborately perfected mechanism for attack, an equally elaborate series of instincts guiding their action to effective purpose; and a complex series of automatic responses to the stimulus afforded by the sight and action of their prey might very well mimic intelligent pursuit and attack, always with certain limits set by the inflexible character of such automatic adjustments. But no animal as large as Tyrannosaurus could leap or spring upon another, and its slow stride quickening into a swift resistless rush, might well end in unavoidable impalement upon the great horns of Triceratops, futile weapons against a small and active enemy, but designed no doubt to meet just such attacks as these. A true picture of these combats of titans of the ancient world we cannot draw; perhaps we will never be able to reconstruct it. But the above considerations may serve to show how widely it would differ from the pictures based upon any modern analogies.

One may well inquire why it is that no such gigantic carnivora have evolved among the mammalian land animals. The largest predaceous quadrupeds living today are the lion and tiger. The bears although some of them are much larger, are not generally carnivorous, except for the polar bear, which is partly aquatic, preying chiefly upon seals and fish. There are indeed carnivorous whales of gigantic size, but no very large land carnivore. There were, it is true, during the Tertiary and Pleistocene, lions and other carnivores considerably larger than the living species. But none of them attained the size of their largest herbivorous contemporaries, or even approached it. Among the dinosaurs on the other hand we find that--setting aside Brontosaurus and its allies as aquatic--the predaceous kinds equalled or exceeded the largest of the herbivorous sorts. The difference is striking, and it does not seem likely that it is merely accidental.

The explanation lies probably in the fact that the large herbivorous mammals are much more intelligent and active, and would be able to use their weapons of defense so as to defy the attacks of relatively slow moving giant beasts of prey, as they do also the more active but less powerful assaults of smaller ones. The elephant or the rhinoceros is in fact practically immune from the attacks of carnivora, and would still be so were the carnivora to increase in size. The large modern carnivora prey upon herbivores of medium or smaller size, which they are active enough to surprise or run down. Carnivora of much larger size would be too slow and heavy in movements to catch small prey, while the larger herbivores by intelligent use of their defensive weapons could still fend them off successfully. In consequence giant carnivores would find no field for action in the Cenozoic world, and hence they have not been evolved.

But the giant herbivorous dinosaurs, well armed or well defended though they were, had not the intelligence to use those weapons effectively under all circumstances. Thus they might be successfully attacked, at least sometimes, by the powerful although slow moving Megalosaurians.

The suggestion has also been made that these giant carnivores were carrion-eaters rather than truly predaceous. The hypothesis can hardly be effectively supported nor attacked. It is presented as a possible alternate.

Albertosaurus. Closely allied to the Tyrannosaurus but smaller, about equal in size to Allosaurus, was the Albertosaurus of the Edmonton formation in Canada. It is somewhat older than the Tyrannosaur although still of the late Cretacic period, and may have been ancestral to it. A fine series of limbs and feet as also skull, tail, etc., are in the Museum's collections. At or about this time carnivorous dinosaurs of slightly smaller size are known to have inhabited New Jersey; a fragmentary skeleton of one secured by Professor Cope in 1869 was described as Laelaps (=Dryptosaurus).[10]

Ornitholestes. In contrast with the Allosaurus and Tyrannosaurus this skeleton represents the smaller and more agile carnivorous dinosaurs which preyed upon the lesser herbivorous reptiles of the period. These little dinosaurs were probably common during all the Age of Reptiles, much as the smaller quadrupeds are today, but skulls or skeletons are rarely found in the formations known to us. The Anchisaurus, Podokesaurus and other genera of the Triassic Period have left innumerable tracks upon the sandy shales of the Newark formation, but only two or three skeletons are known. A cast of one of them is exhibited here. The original is preserved in the Yale Museum. In the succeeding Jurassic Period we have the Compsognathus, smallest of known dinosaurs, and this Ornitholestes some six feet long. A cast of the Compsognathus skeleton is shown, the original found in the lithographic limestone of Solenhofen is preserved in the Munich Museum. The Ornitholestes is from the Bone-Cabin Quarry in Wyoming. The forefoot with its long slender digits is supposed to have been adapted for grasping an active and elusive prey, and the name (Ornitho-lestes = bird-robber) indicates that that prey may sometimes have been the primitive birds which were its contemporaries. In the Cretacic Period, there were also small and medium sized carnivorous dinosaurs, contemporary with the gigantic kinds; a complete skeleton of Ornithomimus at the entrance to the Dinosaur Hall finely illustrates this group. In appearance most of these small dinosaurs must have suggested long-legged bipedal lizards, running and walking on their hind limbs, with the long tail stretched out behind to balance the body. From what we know of their tracks it seems that they walked or ran with a narrow treadway, the footsteps almost in the middle line of progress. They did not hop like perching birds, nor did they waddle like most living reptiles. Occasionally the tail or fore feet touched the ground as they walked; and when they sat down, they rested on the end of the pubic bones and on the tail. So much we can infer from the footprint impressions. The general appearance is shown in the restorations of Ornitholestes, Compsognathus and Anchisaurus by Charles Knight.

Ornithomimus. The skeleton of this animal from the Cretacic of Alberta was found by the Museum expedition of 1914. It is exceptionally complete, and has been mounted as a panel, in position as it lay in the rock, and with considerable parts of the original sandstone matrix still adherent. The long slender limbs, long neck, small head and toothless jaws are all singularly bird-like, and afford a striking contrast to the Tyrannosaurus. At the time of writing, its adaptation and relationships have not yet been thoroughly investigated.

FOOTNOTES:

[Footnote 4: This is still doubtful in Tyrannosaurus. A number of very curious plates were found with one specimen in a quarry. B. Brown, 1913.]

[Footnote 5: Quite recently a series of more or less complete skeletons have been secured from the upper Triassic (Keuper) near Halberstadt in Germany. They are not true Megalosaurians, but primitive types (Pachypodosauria) ancestral to both these and the Sauropoda. Probably many of the Connecticut footprints were made by animals of this primitive group. Anchisaurus certainly belongs to it.]

[Footnote 6: It is evidently "the dinosaur" of Sir Conan Doyle's "Lost World" but the vivid description which the great English novelist gives of its appearance and habits, based probably upon the Hawkins restoration, is not at all in accord with inferences from what is now known of these animals. See p. 44.]

[Footnote 7: Allosaurus, a carnivorous Dinosaur, and its Prey. By W.D. Matthew. Am. Mus. Nat. Hist. Jour. Vol. viii, pp. 3-5, pl. 1.]

[Footnote 8: The cost of preparation is now defrayed by the Museum.]

[Footnote 9: Tyrannosaurus, Restoration and Model of the Skeleton. By Henry Fairfield Osborn. Bull. Amer. Mus. Nat. Hist., 1913, vol. xxxii, art. iv, pp. 91-92.]

[Footnote 10: Since these lines were written the Museum has secured finely preserved skeletons of two or more kinds of Carnivorous Dinosaurs from the Belly River formation in Canada.]

CHAPTER V.

THE AMPHIBIOUS DINOSAURS, BRONTOSAURUS, DIPLODOCUS, ETC.

SUB-ORDER OPISTHOCOELIA (CETIOSAURIA OR SAUROPODA).

These were the Giant Reptiles par-excellence, for all of them were of enormous size, and some were by far the largest of all four-footed animals, exceeded in bulk only by the modern whales. In contrast to the carnivorous dinosaurs these are quadrupedal, with very small head, blunt teeth, long giraffe-like neck, elephantine body and limbs, long massive tail prolonged at the tip into a whip-lash as in the lizards. Like the elephant they have five short toes on each foot, probably buried in life in a large soft pad, but the inner digits bear large claws, blunt like those of turtles, one in the fore foot, three in the hind foot.

To this group belong the Brontosaurus and Diplodocus, the Camarasaurus, Morosaurus and other less known kinds. All of them lived during the late Jurassic and Comanchic ("Lower Cretaceous") and belong to the older of the two principal Dinosaur faunas. They were contemporaries of the Allosaurus and Megalosaurus, the Stegosaurus and Iguanodon, but unlike the Carnivorous and Beaked Dinosaurs they became wholly extinct before the Upper or true Cretacic, and left no relatives to take part in the final epoch of expansion and prosperity of the dinosaurian race at the close of the Reptilian era.

BRONTOSAURUS.

The following description of the Brontosaurus skeleton in the American Museum was first published in the American Museum Journal of April, 1905:[11]

"The Brontosaurus skeleton, the principal feature of the hall, is sixty-six feet eight inches long. (The weight of the animal when alive is estimated by W.K. Gregory at 38 tons). About one-third of the skeleton including the skull is restored in plaster modelled or cast from other incomplete skeletons. The remaining two-thirds belong to one individual, except for a part of the tail, one shoulder-blade and one hind limb, supplied from another skeleton of the same species.

"The skeleton was discovered by Mr. Walter Granger of the Museum expedition of 1898, about nine miles north of Medicine Bow, Wyoming. It took the whole of the succeeding summer to extract it from the rock, pack it, and ship it to the Museum. Nearly two years were consumed in removing the matrix, piecing together and cementing the brittle and shattered petrified bone, strengthening it so that it would bear handling, and restoring the missing parts of the bones in tinted plaster. The articulation and mounting of the skeleton and modelling of the missing bones took an even longer time, so that it was not until February, 1905, that the Brontosaurus was at last ready for exhibition.

"It will appear, therefore, that the collection, preparation and mounting of this gigantic fossil has been a task of extraordinary difficulty. No museum has ever before attempted to mount so large a fossil skeleton, and the great weight and fragile character of the bones made it necessary to devise especial methods to give each bone a rigid and complete support as otherwise it would soon break in pieces from its own weight. The proper articulating of the bones and posing of the limbs were equally difficult problems, for the Amphibious Dinosaurs, to which this animal belongs, disappeared from the earth long before the dawn of the Age of Mammals, and their nearest relatives, the living lizards, crocodiles, etc., are so remote from them in either proportions or habits that they are unsatisfactory guides in determining how the bones were articulated and are of but little use in posing the limbs and other parts of the body in positions that they must have taken during life. Nor among the higher animals of modern times is there one which has any analogy in appearance or habits of life to those which we have been obliged by the study of the skeleton to ascribe to the Brontosaurus.

"As far as the backbone and ribs were concerned, the articulating surfaces of the bones were a sufficient guide to enable us to pose this part of the skeleton properly. The limb joints, however, are so imperfect that we could not in this way make sure of having the bones in a correct position. The following method, therefore, was adopted.

"A dissection and thorough study was made by the writer, with the assistance of Mr. Granger, of the limbs of alligators and other reptiles, and the position, size and action of the principal muscles were carefully worked out. Then the corresponding bones of the Brontosaurus were studied, and the position and size of the corresponding muscles were worked out, so far as they could be recognized from the scars and processes preserved on the bone. The Brontosaurus limbs were then provisionally articulated and posed, and the position and size of each muscle were represented by a broad strip of paper extending from its origin to its insertion. The action and play of the muscles on the limb of the Brontosaurus could then be studied, and the bones adjusted until a proper and mechanically correct pose was reached. The limbs were then permanently mounted in these poses, and the skeleton as it stands is believed to represent, as nearly as study of the fossil enables us to know, a characteristic position that the animal actually assumed during life....

"In proportions and appearance the Brontosaurus was quite unlike any living animal. It had a long thick tail like the lizards and crocodiles, a long, flexible neck like an ostrich, a thick short, slab-sided body and straight, massive, post-like limbs suggesting the elephant, and a remarkably small head for the size of the beast. The ribs, limb-bones and tail-bones are exceptionally solid and heavy; the vertebrae of the back and neck, and the skull, on the contrary are constructed so as to combine the minimum of weight with the large surface necessary for the attachment of the huge muscles, the largest possible articulating surfaces, and the necessary strength at all points of strain. For this purpose they are constructed with an elaborate system of braces and buttresses of thin bony plates connecting the broad articulating surfaces and muscular attachments, all the bone between these thin plates being hollowed into a complicated system of air-cavities. This remarkable structure can be best seen in the unmounted skeleton of Camarasaurus, another Amphibious Dinosaur." (The scientific name Camarasaurus=chambered lizard, has reference to this peculiarity of construction.)

"The teeth of the Brontosaurus indicate that it was an herbivorous animal, feeding on soft vegetable food. Three opinions as to the habitat of Amphibious Dinosaurs have been held by scientific authorities. The first, advocated by Professor Owen, who described the first specimens found sixty years ago (1841-60) and supported especially by Professor Cope, has been most generally adopted. This regards the animals as spending their lives entirely in shallow water, partly immersed, wading about on the bottom, or perhaps occasionally swimming, but unable to emerge entirely upon dry land.[12] More recently, Professor Osborn has advocated the view that they resorted occasionally to the land for egg laying or other purposes, and still more recently the view has been taken by Mr. Riggs and the late Professor Hatcher that they were chiefly terrestrial animals. The writer inclines to the view of Owen and Cope, whose unequalled knowledge of comparative anatomy renders their opinion on this doubtful question especially authoritative.

"The contrast between the massive structure of the limb-bones, ribs and tail, and the light construction of the backbone, neck and skull, suggests that the animal was amphibious, living chiefly in shallow water, where it could wade about on the bottom, feeding upon the abundant vegetation of the coastal swamps and marshes, and pretty much out of reach of the powerful and active Carnivorous Dinosaurs which were its principal enemies. The water would buoy up the massive body and prevent its weight from pressing too heavily on the imperfect joints of the limb and foot bones, which were covered during life with thick cartilage, like the joints of whales, sea-lizards and other aquatic animals. If the full weight of the animal came on these imperfect joints the cartilage would yield and the ends of the bones would grind against each other, thus preventing the limb from moving without tearing the joint to pieces. The massive, solid limb and foot bones weighted the limbs while immersed in water, and served the same purpose as the lead in a diver's shoes, enabling the Brontosaurus to walk about firmly and securely under water. On the other hand, the joints of the neck and back are exceptionally broad, well fitting and covered with a much thinner surface of cartilage. The pressure was thus much better distributed over the joint, and the full weight of the part of the animal above water (reduced as it was by the cellular construction of the bones) might be borne on these joints without the cartilage giving way.

"Looking at the mounted skeleton we may see that if a line be drawn from the hip joint to the shoulder-blade, all the bones below this are massive, all above (including neck and head) are lightly constructed. This line may be taken to indicate the average water-line, so to speak, of this Leviathan of the Shallows. The long neck would enable the animal, however, to wade to a considerable depth, and it might forage for food either in the branches or the tops of trees, or more probably, among the soft succulent water-plants of the bottom. The row of short spoon-shaped stubby teeth around the front of the mouth would serve to bite or pull off soft leaves and water-plants, but the animal evidently could not masticate its food, and must have swallowed it without chewing as do modern reptiles and birds.

"The brain-case occupies only a small part of the back of the skull, so that the brain must have been small even for a reptile, and its organization (as inferred from the form of the brain-case) indicates a very low grade of intelligence. Much larger than the brain proper was the spinal cord, especially in the region of the sacrum, controlling most of the reflex and involuntary actions of the huge organism. Hence we can best regard the Brontosaurus as a great, slow-moving animal automaton, a vast storehouse of organized matter directed chiefly or solely by instinct, and to a very limited degree, if at all, by conscious intelligence. Its huge size and its imperfect organization, compared with the great quadrupeds of today, rendered its movements slow and clumsy; its small and low brain shows that it must have been automatic, instinctive and unintelligent."

Composition of the Brontosaurus Skeleton. "The principal specimen, No. 460, is from the Nine Mile Crossing of the Little Medicine Bow River, Wyoming. It consists of the 5th, 6th, and 8th to 13th cervical vertebrae, 1st to 9th dorsal and 3rd to 19th caudal vertebrae, all the ribs, both coracoids, parts of sacrum and ilia, both ischia and pubes, left femur and astragalus, and part of left fibula. The backbone and most of the neck of this specimen were found articulated together in the quarry, the ribs of one side in position, the remainder of the bones scattered around them, and some of the tail bones weathered out on the surface.

"From No. 222, found at Como Bluffs, Wyo., were supplied the right scapula, 10th dorsal vertebra, and right femur and tibia.

"No. 339, from Bone-Cabin Quarry, Wyoming, supplied the 20th to 40th caudal vertebrae, No. 592, from the same locality the metatarsals of the right hind foot; and a few toe bones are supplied from other specimens.

"The remainder of the skeleton is modelled in plaster, the scapula, humerus, radius and ulna from the skeleton in the Yale Museum, the rest principally from specimens in our own collections. The modelling of the skull is based partly upon specimens in the Yale Museum, but principally upon the complete skull of Morosaurus shown in another case.

"Mounted by A. Hermann, completed Feb. 10, 1905."

Diplodocus. The Diplodocus nearly equalled the Brontosaurus in bulk and exceeded it in length. A skeleton in the Carnegie Museum at Pittsburgh measures 87 feet in total length; although the mount is composed from several individuals these proportions are probably not far from correct. The skull is smaller and differently shaped and the teeth are of quite different type. In the American Museum of Natural History, a partial skeleton is exhibited in the wall case to the left of the entrance of the Dinosaur Hall, and in an A-case near by are skulls of Diplodocus and Morosaurus and a model of the skull of Brontosaurus. The Diplodocus skull is widely different from the other two in size and proportions and in the characters of teeth.

When the first remains of these amphibious Dinosaurs were found in the Oxford Clays of England, they were considered by Richard Owen to be related to the Crocodiles, and named Opisthocoelia. Subsequently the finding of complete skeletons in this country led Cope and Marsh to place them with the true Dinosaurs and the latter named them Sauropoda.[13] Remains of these animals have also been found in India, in German East Africa, in Madagascar, and in South America, so that they were evidently widely distributed. In the Northern world they survived until the Comanchic or Lower Cretaceous Period, but in the southern continents they may have lived on into the Upper Cretaceous or true Cretacic. Some of the remains recently found in German East Africa indicate an animal exceeding either Brontosaurus or Diplodocus in bulk.

At the date of writing this handbook only preliminary accounts have been given of the marvellous finds made near Tendaguru by the expedition from Berlin. From these it appears that in length of neck and fore limb this East African Dinosaur greatly exceeded either Brontosaurus or Diplodocus. The hinder parts of the skeleton however, were relatively small. The proportions and measurements given tally closely with the American Brachiosaurus, a gigantic sauropod whose incomplete remains are preserved in the Field Museum in Chicago and to this genus the Berlin authorities now refer their largest and finest skeleton. If the Berlin specimens are correctly referred to Brachiosaurus they indicate an animal somewhat exceeding Diplodocus or Brontosaurus in total bulk but distinguished by much longer fore limbs and an immensely long neck--a giraffe-like wader adapted to take refuge in deeper waters, more out of reach of the fierce carnivores of the land.[14]

FOOTNOTES:

[Footnote 11: The mounted Skeleton of Brontosaurus, by W.D. Matthew,

Amer. Mus. Jour. Vol. v, pp. 63-70, figs. 1-5.]

[Footnote 12: Professor Williston makes the following criticism of this theory:

"I cannot agree with this view--the animals must have laid their eggs upon land--for the reason that reptile eggs cannot hatch in water. S.W.W."

But with deference to Williston's high authority I may note that there is no evidence that the Sauropoda were egg-laying reptiles. They, or some of them, may have been viviparous like the Ichthyosaurus.]

[Footnote 13: European palaeontologists, especially Huxley and Seeley in England, had also recognized their true relationships, and Seeley's term Cetiosauria has precedence over Sauropoda, although the latter is in common use.]

[Footnote 14: It is of interest to observe that in this group of Sauropoda, the Brachiosaurid? the neural spines of the vertebrae are much simpler and narrower than in the Brontosaurus and Diplodocus. The attachments were thus less extensive for the muscles of the back, indicating that these muscles were less powerful. This difference is correlated by Professor Williston with the longer fore limbs of the Brachiosaurus, as signifying that the animal was less able, as indeed he had less need, to rise up upon the hind limbs, in comparison with Diplodocus or Brontosaurus in which the fore limbs were relatively short.]

CHAPTER VI.

THE BEAKED DINOSAURS.

ORDER ORTHOPODA (ORNITHISCHIA OR PREDENTATA.)

The peculiar feature of this group of Dinosaurs is the horny beak or bill. The bony core sutured to the front of the upper and lower jaws was covered in life by a horny sheath, as in birds or turtles. But this is not the only feature in which they came nearer to birds than do the other Dinosaurs. The pelvic or hip bones are much more bird-like in many respects, especially the backward direction of the pubic bone, the presence of a prepubis, in the number of vertebrae co 䰩 sified into a solid sacrum, in the proportions of the ilium and so on. Various features in the anatomy of the head, shoulder-blades and hind limbs are equally suggestive of birds, and it seems probable that the earliest ancestors of the birds were very closely related to the ancestors of this group of Dinosaurs. But the ancestral birds became adapted to flying, the ancestral Predentates to terrestrial life, and in their later development became as widely diversified in form and habits as the warm-blooded quadrupeds which succeeded them in the Age of Mammals.

These Beaked Dinosaurs were, so far as we can tell, all vegetarians. Unlike the birds, they retained their teeth and in some cases converted them into a grinding apparatus which served the same purpose as the grinders of herbivorous quadrupeds. It is interesting to observe the different way in which this result is attained. In the mammals the teeth, originally more complex in construction and fewer in number, are converted into efficient grinders by infolding and elongation of the crown of each tooth so as to produce on the wearing surface a complex pattern of enamel ridges with softer dentine or cement intervening, making a series of crests and hollows continually renewed during the wear of the tooth. In the reptile the teeth, originally simple in construction but more numerous and continually renewed as they wear down and fall out,[15] are banked up in several close packed rows, the enamel borders and softer dentine giving a wearing surface of alternating crests and hollows continually renewed, and reinforced from time to time, by the addition of new rows of teeth to one side, as the first formed rows wear down to the roots. This is the best illustrated in the Trachodon (see fig. 27); the other groups have not so perfect a mechanism.

A. THE IGUANODONTS: IGUANODON, CAMPTOSAURUS.

Sub-Order Ornithopoda or Iguanodontia.

In the early days of geology, about the middle of the nineteenth century, bones and footprints of huge extinct reptiles were found in the rocks of the Weald in south-eastern England. They were described by Mantell and Owen and shown to pertain to an extinct group of reptiles which Owen called the Dinosauria. So different were these bones from those of any modern reptiles that even the anatomical learning of the great English palaeontologist did not enable him to place them all correctly or reconstruct the true proportions of the animal to which they belonged. With them were found associated the bones of the great carnivorous dinosaur Megalosaurus; and the weird reconstructions of these animals, based by Waterhouse Hawkins upon the imperfect knowledge and erroneous ideas then prevailing, must be familiar to many of the older readers of this handbook. Life size restorations of these and other extinct animals were erected in the grounds of the Crystal Palace at Sydenham, London, and in Central Park, New York. Those in London still exist, so far as the writer is aware, but the stern mandate of a former mayor of New York ordered the destruction of the Central Park models, not indeed as incorrect scientifically, but as inconsistent with the doctrines of revealed religion, and they were accordingly broken up and thrown into the waters of the Park lake. Small replicas of these early attempts at restoring dinosaurs may still be seen in some of the older museums in this country and abroad.

The real construction of the Iguanodon was gradually built up by later discoveries, and in 1877 an extraordinary find in a coal mine at Bernissart in Belgium brought to light no less than seventeen skeletons more or less complete. These were found in an ancient fissure filled with rocks of Comanchic age, traversing the Carboniferous strata in which the coal seam lay, and with them were skeletons of other extinct reptiles of smaller size. The open fissure had evidently served as a trap into which these ancient giants had fallen, and either killed by the fall or unable to escape from the pit, their remains had been subsequently covered up by sediments and the pit filled in to remain sealed up until the present day. These skeletons, unique in their occurrence and manner of discovery, are the pride of the Brussels Museum of Natural History, and, together with the earlier discoveries, have made the Iguanodon the most familiar type of dinosaur to the people of England and Western Europe.

Camptosaurus. The American counterpart of the Iguanodons of Europe was the Camptosaurus, nearly related and generally similar in proportions but including mostly smaller species, and lacking some of the peculiar features of the Old World genus. In the National Museum at Washington, are mounted two skeletons of Camptosaurus, a large and a small species, and in the American Museum a skeleton of a small species. It suggests a large kangaroo in size and proportions, but the three-toed feet, with hoof-like claws, the reptilian skull, loosely put together, with lizard-like cheek teeth and turtle beak indicate a near relative of the great Iguanodon.

Thescelosaurus. The Iguanodont family survived until the close of the Age of Reptiles, with no great change in proportions or characters. Its latest member is Thescelosaurus, a contemporary of Triceratops. Partial skeletons of this animal are shown in the Dinosaur Hall; a more complete one is in the National Museum.

FOOTNOTES:

[Footnote 15: Trachodont teeth never drop out, they are completely consumed. Only in the Iguanodonts and Ceratopsia are they shed.--B. Brown.]

CHAPTER VII.

THE BEAKED DINOSAURS (Continued).

B. THE DUCK BILLED DINOSAURS,--TRACHODON, SAUROLOPHUS, ETC.

Sub-Order Ornithopoda; Family Trachodontid?

These animals of the Upper Cretaceous are probably descended from the Iguanodonts of an older period. But the long ages that intervened, some millions of years, have brought about various changes in the race, not so much in general proportions as in altering the form and relations of various bones of skull and skeleton and perfecting their adaptation to a somewhat different habit of life, so that they must be regarded as descendants perhaps, but certainly rather distant relatives, of the older group.

We know more about the Trachodonts than any other dinosaurs. For not only are the skeletons more frequently found articulated, but parts of the skin are not uncommonly preserved with them, and in one specimen at least, so much of the skin is preserved that it may fairly be called a "dinosaur mummy." This specimen of Trachodon is in the American Museum, and beside it are two fine mounted skeletons of the largest size. There is also on exhibition a panel mount of a nearly related genus, Saurolophus the skeleton lying as it was found in the rock, and a fine skeleton of a third genus Corythosaurus with the skin partly preserved on both sides of the crushed and flattened body stands beside it. In the Tyrannosaurus group when completed will appear a fourth skeleton of the Trachodon. Several skulls and incomplete skeletons on exhibition and other skeletons not yet prepared add to the Museum collection of this group. Trachodon skeletons may also be found in the Museums of New Haven, Washington, Frankfurt-on-the-Main, London and Paris, but nowhere a series comparable to that displayed at the American Museum.

THE TRACHODON GROUP.

The following description of the Trachodon group is by Mr. Barnum Brown and first appeared in the American Museum Journal for April 1908:[16]

"This group takes us back in imagination to the Cretaceous period, more than three millions of years ago, when Trachodonts were among the most numerous of the dinosaurs. Two members of the family are represented here as feeding in the marshes that characterized the period, when one is startled by the approach of a carnivorous dinosaur, Tyrannosaurus, their enemy, and rises on tiptoe to look over the surrounding plants and determine the direction from which it is coming. The other Trachodon, unaware of danger, continues peacefully to crop the foliage. Perhaps the erect member of the group had already had unpleasant experiences with hostile beasts, for a bone of its left foot bears three sharp gashes which were made by the teeth of some carnivorous dinosaur.

"By thus grouping the skeletons in lifelike attitudes, the relation of the different bones can best be shown, but these of course are only two of the attitudes commonly taken by the creatures during life. Mechanical and anatomical considerations, especially the long straight shafts of the leg bones, indicate that dinosaurs walked with their limbs straight under the body, rather than in a crawling attitude with the belly close to the ground, as is common among living reptiles.

"Trachodonts lived near the close of the Age of Reptiles in the Upper Cretaceous and had a wide geographical distribution, their remains having been found in New Jersey, Mississippi and Alabama, but more commonly in Wyoming, Montana, and the Dakotas. A suggestion of the great antiquity of these specimens is given by the fact that since the animals died layers of rock aggregating many thousand feet in vertical thickness have been deposited along the Atlantic coast.

"The bones of the erect specimen are but little crushed and a clear conception of the proportions of the animal can best be obtained from this specimen. It will be seen that the Trachodon was shaped somewhat like a kangaroo, with short fore legs, long hind legs, and a long tail. The fore limbs are reduced indeed to about one-sixth the size of the hind limbs and judging from the size and shape of the foot bones the front legs could not have borne much weight. They were probably used in supporting the anterior portion of the body when the creature was feeding, and in aiding it to recover an upright position. The specimen represented as feeding is posed so that the fore legs carry very little of the weight of the body. There are four toes on the front foot but the thumb is greatly reduced and the fifth digit or little finger, is absent." (Subsequent discoveries have shown that the arrangement of the digits made by Marsh and followed in this skeleton is incorrect. It is the first digit that is absent, and the fifth is reduced.)

"The hind legs are massive and have three well developed toes ending in broad hoofs. The pelvis is lightly constructed with bones elongated like those of birds. The long deep compressed tail was particularly adapted for locomotion in the water. It may also have served to balance the creature when standing erect on shore. The broad expanded lip of bone known as the fourth trochanter, on the inner posterior face of the femur or thigh bone was for the attachment of powerful tail muscles similar to those which enable the crocodile to move its tail from side to side with such dexterity. This trochanter is absent from the thigh bones of land-inhabiting dinosaurs with short tails, such as Stegosaurus and Triceratops. The tail muscles were attached to the vertebrae by numerous rod-like tendons which are preserved in position as fossils on the erect skeleton. Trachodonts are thought to have been expert swimmers. Unlike other dinosaurs their remains are frequently found in rocks that were formed under sea water probably bordering the shores but nevertheless containing typical sea shells.

"The elaborate dental apparatus is such as to show clearly that Trachodonts were strictly herbivorous creatures. The mouth was expanded to form a broad duck-like bill which during life was covered with a horny sheath, as in birds and turtles. Each jaw is provided with from 45 to 60 vertical and from 10 to 14 horizontal rows of teeth, so that there were more than 2000 teeth altogether in both jaws.

"Among living saurians, or reptiles, the small South American iguana Amblyrhynchus may be compared in some respects with the Trachodons notwithstanding the difference in size. These modern saurians live in great numbers on the shores of the Galapagos Islands off the coast of Chile. They swim out to sea in shoals and feed exclusively on seaweed which grows on the bottom at some distance from shore. The animal swims with perfect ease and quickness by a serpentine movement of its body and flattened tail, its legs meanwhile being closely pressed to its side and motionless. This is also the method of propulsion of crocodiles when swimming.

"The carnivorous or flesh-eating dinosaurs that lived on land, such as Allosaurus and Tyrannosaurus, were protected from foes by their sharp biting teeth, while the land-living herbivorous forms were provided with defensive horns, as in Triceratops, sharp spines as in Stegosaurus or were completely armored as in Ankylosaurus. Trachodon was not provided with horns, spines or plated armor, but it was sufficiently protected from carnivorous land forms by being able to enter and remain in the water. Its skin was covered with small raised scales, pentagonal in form on the body and tail, where they were largest, with smaller reticulations over the joints but never overlapping as in snakes or fishes. A Trachodon skeleton was recently found with an impression of the skin surrounding the vertebrae which is so well preserved that it gives even the contour of the tail as is shown in the illustration (fig. 32).

"During the existence of the Trachodonts the climate of the northern part of North America was much warmer than it is at present, the plant remains indicating a climate for Wyoming and Montana similar to what now prevails in Southern California. Palm leaves resembling the palmetto of Florida are frequently found in the same rocks with these skeletons. Here occur also such, at present, widely separated trees as the gingko now native of China, and the Sequoia now native of the Pacific Coast. Fruits and leaves of the fig tree are also common, but most abundant among the plant remains are the Equisetae or horsetail rushes, some species of which possibly supplied the Trachodons with food.

[Illustration: Fig. 29.--Restoration of the Duck-billed Dinosaur Trachodon. This restoration, made by Mr. Knight under supervision of Professor Osborn, embodies the latest evidence as to the structure and characteristic poses of these animals, the character of the skin and their probable habits and environment. After Osborn]

"Impressions of the more common plants found in the rocks of this period with sections of the tree trunks showing the woody structure will be [have been] introduced into the group as the ground on which the skeletons stand. In the rivers and bayous of that remote period there also lived many kinds of Unios or fresh-water clams, and other shells, the casts of which are frequently found with Trachodon bones. The fossil trunk of a coniferous tree was found in Wyoming, which was filled with groups of wood-living shells similar to the living Teredo. These also will be introduced in the ground-work.

"The skeleton mounted in a feeding posture was one of the principal specimens in the Cope Collection, which, through the generosity of the late President Jesup, was purchased and given to the American Museum. It was found near the Moreau River, north of the Black Hills, South Dakota, in 1882, by Dr. J.L. Wortman and Mr. R.S. Hill, collectors for Professor Cope. The erect skeleton came from Crooked Creek, central Montana, and was found by a ranchman, Mr. Oscar Hunter, while riding through the bad lands with a companion in 1904. The specimen was partly exposed, with backbone and ribs united in position. The parts that were weathered out are much lighter in color than the other bones. Their large size caused some discussion between the ranchmen and to settle the question, Mr. Hunter dismounted and kicked off all the tops of the vertebrae and rib-heads above ground, thereby proving by their brittle nature that they were stone and not buffalo bones as the other man contended. The proof was certainly conclusive, but it was extremely exasperating to the subsequent collectors. Another ranchman, Mr. Alfred Sensiba, heard of the find and knowing that it was valuable 'traded' Mr. Hunter a six-shooter for his interest in it. The specimen was purchased from Messrs. Sensiba Brothers and excavated by the American Museum in 1906."

THE DINOSAUR "MUMMY."

We all believe that the Dinosaurs existed. But to realize it is not so easy. Even with the help of the mounted skeletons and restorations, they are somewhat unreal and shadowy beings in the minds of most of us. But this "dinosaur mummy" sprawling on his back and covered with shrunken skin--a real specimen, not restored in any part--brings home the reality of this ancient world even as the mummy of an ancient Egyptian brings home to us the reality of the world of the Pharaohs. The description of this unique skeleton by Professor Henry Fairfield Osborn first appeared in the Museum Journal for January 1911.[17]

"Two years ago (1908) through the Jesup Fund, the Museum came into possession of a most unique specimen discovered in August 1908, by the veteran fossil hunter Charles H. Sternberg of Kansas. It is a large herbivorous dinosaur of the closing period of the Age of Reptiles and is known to palaeontologists as Trachodon or more popularly as the 'duck-billed dinosaur.'

"The skeleton or hard parts of these very remarkable animals had been known for over forty years, and a few specimens of the epidermal covering, but it was not until the discovery of the Sternberg specimen that a complete knowledge of the outer covering of these dinosaurs was gained. It appears probable that in a number of cases these priceless skin impressions were mostly destroyed in removing the fossil specimens from their surroundings because the explorers were not expecting to find anything of the kind. Altogether seven specimens have been discovered in which these delicate skin impressions were partly preserved, but the 'Trachodon mummy' far surpasses all the others, as it yields a nearly complete picture of the outer covering.

"The reason the Sternberg specimen (Trachodon annectens) may be known as a dinosaur 'mummy' is that in all the parts of the animal which are preserved (i.e. all except the hind limbs and the tail), the epidermis is shrunken around the limbs, tightly drawn along the bony surfaces, and contracted like a great curtain below the chest area. This condition of the epidermis suggests the following theory of the deposition and preservation of this wonderful specimen, namely: that after dying a natural death the animal was not attacked or preyed upon by its enemies, and the body lay exposed to the sun entirely undisturbed for a long time, perhaps upon a broad sand flat of a stream in the low-water stage; the muscles and viscera thus became completely dehydrated, or desiccated by the action of the sun, the epidermis shrank around the limbs, was tightly drawn down along all the bony surfaces, and became hardened and leathery, on the abdominal surfaces the epidermis was certainly drawn within the body cavity, while it was thrown into creases and folds along the sides of the body owing to the shrinkage of the tissues within. At the termination of a possible low-water season during which these processes of desiccation took place, the 'mummy' may have been caught in a sudden flood, carried down the stream and rapidly buried in a bed of fine river sand intermingled with sufficient elements of clay to take a perfect cast or mold of all the epidermal markings before any of the epidermal tissues had time to soften under the solvent action of the water. In this way the markings were indicated with absolute distinctness, ... the visitor will be able by the use of the hand glass to study even the finer details of the pattern, although of course there is no trace either of the epidermis itself, which has entirely disappeared, or of the pigmentation or coloring, if such existed.

"Although attaining a height of fifteen to sixteen feet the trachodons were not covered with scales or a bony protecting armature, but with dermal tubercles of relatively small size, which varied in shape and arrangement in different species, and not improbably associated with this varied epidermal pattern there was a varied color pattern. The theory of a color pattern is based chiefly upon the fact that the larger tubercles concentrate and become more numerous on all those portions of the body exposed to the sun, that is, on the outer surfaces of the fore and hind limbs, and appear to increase also along the sides of the body and to be more concentrated on the back. On the less exposed areas, the under side of the body and the inner sides of the limbs, the smaller tubercles are more numerous, the larger tubercles being reduced to small irregularly arranged patches. From analogy with existing lizards and snakes we may suppose, therefore, that the trachodons presented a darker appearance when seen from the back and a lighter appearance when seen from the front.

"The thin character of the epidermis as revealed by this specimen favors also the theory that these animals spent a large part of their time in the water, which theory is strengthened by the fact that the diminutive fore limb terminates not in claws or hoofs, but in a broad extension of the skin, reaching beyond the fingers and forming a kind of paddle.[18] The marginal web which connects all the fingers with each other, together with the fact that the lower side of the fore limb is as delicate in its epidermal structure as the upper, certainly tends to support the theory of the swimming rather than the walking or terrestrial function of this fore paddle as indicated in the accompanying preliminary restoration that was made by Charles R. Knight working under the writer's direction. One is drawn in the conventional bipedal or standing posture while the other is in a quadrupedal pose or walking position, sustaining or balancing the fore part of the body on a muddy surface with its fore feet. In the distant water a large number of animals are disporting themselves.

"The designation of these animals as the 'duck-billed' dinosaurs in reference to the broadening of the beak, has long been considered in connection with the theory of aquatic habitat. The conversion of the fore limb into a sort of paddle, as evidenced by the Sternberg specimen, strengthens this theory.

"This truly wonderful specimen, therefore, nearly doubles our previous insight into the habits and life of a very remarkable group of reptiles."

Saurolophus, Corythosaurus. In the latest Cretaceous formation, the Lance or Triceratops beds, all the duck-billed dinosaurs are much alike, and are referred to the single genus Trachodon. In somewhat older formations of the Cretacic period there were several different kinds. Saurolophus has a high bony spine rising from the top of the skull; in Corythosaurus there is a thin high crest like the crown of a cassowary on top of the skull, and the muzzle is short and small giving a very peculiar aspect to the head. Complete skeletons of these two genera are exhibited in the Dinosaur Hall; the Corythosaurus is worthy of careful study, as the skin of the body, hind limbs and tail, the ossified tendons, and even the impressions of the muscular tissues in parts of the body and tail, are more or less clearly indicated.

These Duck-billed Dinosaurs probably ranged all over North America and the northerly portions of the Old World during the later Cretacic. Fragmentary remains have been found in New Jersey and southward along the Atlantic coast. A partial skeleton was described many years ago by Leidy under the name of Hadrosaurus and restored and mounted in the museum of the Philadelphia Academy of Sciences. Telmatosaurus of the Gosau formation in Austria also belongs to this group, and fragmentary remains have been found in the upper Cretacic of Belgium, England and France.

FOOTNOTES:

[Footnote 16: Brown, Barnum. "The Trachodon Group." Amer. Mus. Jour. Vol. viii, pp. 51-56, plate and 3 text figs., 1908.]

[Footnote 17: Osborn, Henry Fairfield, "Dinosaur Mummy" Amer. Mus. Jour. Vol. xi, pp. 7-11, illustrated, Jan. 1911.]

[Footnote 18: There is some doubt whether this was really the condition during life. W.D.M.]

CHAPTER VIII.

THE BEAKED DINOSAURS (Continued.)

C. THE ARMORED DINOSAURS--STEGOSAURUS, ANKYLOSAURUS.

Sub-Order Stegosauria.

This group of dinosaurs is most remarkable for the massive bony armor plates, crests or spines covering the body and tail. They were more or less completely quadrupedal instead of bipedal, with straight post-like limbs and short rounded hoofed feet adapted to support the weight of the massive body and heavy armature. Although so different superficially from the bird-footed biped Iguanodonts they are evidently related to them, for the teeth are similar, and the horny beak, the construction of the pelvis, the three-toed hind foot and four-toed front foot all betray relationship. From what we know of them it seems probable that they evolved from Iguanodont ancestors, developing the bony armor as a protection against the attacks of carnivorous dinosaurs, and modifying the proportions of limbs and feet to enable them to support its weight. They were evidently herbivorous and some of them of gigantic size. Smaller kinds with less massive armor have been found in Europe but the largest and most extraordinary members of this strange race are from North America.

STEGOSAURUS.

This extraordinary reptile equalled the Allosaurus in size, and bore along the crest of the back a double row of enormous bony plates projecting upward and somewhat outward alternately to one side and the other. The largest of these plates situated just back of the pelvis were over two feet high, two and a half long, thinning out from a base four inches thick. The tail was armed with four or more stout spines two feet long and five or six inches thick at the base. In the neck region and probably elsewhere the skin had numerous small bony nodules and some larger ones imbedded in its substance or protecting its surface. The head was absurdly small for so huge an animal, and the stiff thick tail projected backward but was not long enough to reach the ground. The hind limbs are very long and straight, the fore limbs relatively short, and the short high arched back and extremely deep and compressed body served to exaggerate the height and prominence of the great plates. The surface of these plates, covered with a network of blood-vessels, shows that they bore a covering of thick horny skin during life, which probably projected as a ridge beyond their edges and still further increased their size. The spines of the tail, also, were probably cased in horn.

This extraordinary animal was a contemporary of the Brontosaurus and Allosaurus, and its discovery was one of the great achievements of the late Professor Marsh. The skeletons which he described are mounted in the Yale and National Museums. Another skeleton was found in the famous Bone-Cabin Quarry, near Medicine Bow, Wyoming, by the American Museum Expedition of 1901. This skeleton, at present withdrawn from lack of space, will be mounted in the Jurassic Dinosaur Hall in the new wing now under construction.

ANKYLOSAURUS.

Related to Stegosaurus, equally huge, but very different in proportions and character of its armor was the Ankylosaurus of the late Cretacic. This animal, a contemporary of the Tyrannosaurus and duck-billed dinosaurs was more effectively though less grotesquely armored than its more ancient relative. The body is covered with massive bony plates set close together and lying flat over the surface from head to tip of tail. While the stegosaur's body was narrow and compressed, in this animal it is exceptionally broad and the wide spreading ribs are co 輻 sified with the vertebrae, making a very solid support for the transverse rows of armor plates. The head is broad triangular, flat topped and solidly armored, the plates consolidated with the surface of the skull and overhanging sides and front, the nostrils and eyes overhung by plates and bosses of bone; and the tail ended in a blunt heavy club of massive plates consolidated to each other and to the tip of the tail vertebrae. The legs were short, massive and straight, ending probably in elephant-like feet. The animal has well been called "the most ponderous animated citadel the world has ever seen" and we may suppose that when it tucked in its legs and settled down on the surface it would be proof even against the attacks of the terrible Tyrannosaur.

This marvellous animal was made known to science by the discoveries of the Museum parties in Montana and Alberta under Barnum Brown. Fragmentary remains of smaller relatives had been discovered by earlier explorers but nothing that gave any adequate notion of its character or gigantic size. From a partial skeleton discovered in the Hell Creek beds of Montana, and others in the Edmonton and Belly River formations of the Red Deer River, Alberta, it has been possible to reconstruct the entire skeleton of the animal, save for the feet, and to locate and arrange most of the armor plates exactly. A skeleton mount from these specimens will shortly be constructed for the Cretaceous Dinosaur Hall.

Scelidosaurus, Polacanthus, etc. Various armored dinosaurs, of smaller size and less heavily plated, have been described from the Jurassic, Comanchic and Cretacic formations of Europe. The best known are Scelidosaurus of the Lower Jurassic of England, and Polacanthus of the Comanchic (Wealden). Stegopelta of the Cretaceous of Wyoming is more nearly related to Ankylosaurus.

CHAPTER IX.

THE BEAKED DINOSAURS (Concluded.)

D. THE HORNED DINOSAURS, TRICERATOPS, ETC.

Sub-Order Ceratopsia.

In 1887 Professor Marsh published a brief notice of what he supposed to be a fossil bison horn found near Denver, Colorado. Two years later the explorations of the lamented John B. Hatcher in Wyoming and Montana resulted in the unexpected discovery that this horn belonged not to a bison but to a gigantic horned reptile, and that it belonged not in the geological yesterday as at first thought, but in the far back Cretacic, millions of years ago. For Mr. Hatcher found complete skulls, and later secured skeletons, clearly of the Dinosaurian group, but representing a race of dinosaurs whose existence, or at least their extraordinary character, had been quite unsuspected. It appeared indeed that certain teeth and skeleton bones previously discovered by Professor Cope were related to this new type of dinosaur, but the fragments known to the Philadelphia professor gave him no idea of what the animal was like, although with his usual acumen he had discerned that they differed from any animal known to science and registered them as new under the names of Agathaumas 1873 and Monoclonius 1876. Professor Marsh re-named his supposed bison "Ceratops" (i.e. "horned face") and gave to the closely related skulls discovered by Mr. Hatcher the name of Triceratops (i.e. "three horned face"), while to the whole group he gave the name of Ceratopsia.

These were the first of a long series of discoveries which through scientific and popular descriptions have made the Horned Dinosaurs familiar to the world. Most of them are still very imperfectly known, and of their evolution and earlier history we know very little as yet. But we can form a fairly correct idea of their general appearance and habits and of the part they played in the world of the late Cretacic. So far as known they were limited to North America. The most striking feature of the Horned Dinosaurs is the gigantic skull, armed with a pair of horns over the orbits and a median horn on the nasal bones in front, and with a great bony crest projecting at the back and sides. In some species the skull with its bony frill attains a length of seven or even eight feet and about three feet width; the usual length is five or six feet and the width about three. In the best known genus, Triceratops, the paired horns are long and stout and the front horn quite short or almost absent, while in Monoclonius these proportions are reversed, the front horn being long while the paired horns are rudimentary.

The teeth are in a single row but are broadened out into a wide grinding surface. The animal was quadrupedal, with short massive limbs and rounded elephantine feet tipped with hoofs, three in the hind foot, four in the fore foot, a short massive tail that could hardly reach the ground, a short broad-barrelled body and a short neck completely hidden on top and sides by the overhanging bony frill of the skull. In many respects these animals are suggestive far more than any other dinosaurs, of the great quadrupeds of

Tertiary and modern times, rhinoceroses, hippopotami, titanotheres and elephants, as in the horns they suggest the bison. For this reason although less gigantic than the Brontosaurus or Tyrannosaurus, less grotesque perhaps, than the Stegosaurus, they are more interesting than any other dinosaurs. While thus departing far from the earlier type of the beaked dinosaurs (the Iguanodonts) they are evidently descended from them.

TRICERATOPS.

This is the best known of the Horned Dinosaurs, as various skulls and partial skeletons have been found from which it has been possible to reconstruct the entire animal. There is a mounted skeleton in the National Museum, another will shortly be mounted in the American Museum, and there are skulls in several American and European museums.

Triceratops exceeded the largest rhinoceroses in bulk, equalling a fairly large elephant, but with much shorter legs. The great horns over the eyes projected forward or partly upward; in one of our skulls they are 33-1/2 inches long. During life they were probably covered with horn increasing the length by six inches or perhaps a foot. The ball-like condyle for articulation of the neck lies far underneath, at the base of the frill, almost in the middle of the skull.

Monoclonius, Ceratops, etc. The Triceratops and another equally gigantic Horned Dinosaur, Torosaurus, were the last survivors of their race. In somewhat older formations of Cretacic age are found remains of smaller kinds, some of them ancestors of these latest survivors, others collaterally related. None of these have the bony frill completely roofing over the neck as it does in Triceratops. There is always a central spine projecting backwards and widening out at the top to the bony margin of the frill which sweeps around on each side to join bony plates that project from the sides of the skull top. This encloses an open space or "fenestra," so that the neck was not completely protected above. Sometimes the margin of the frill is plain, at other times it carries a number of great spikes, like a gigantic Horned Lizard (Phrynosoma).

In Ceratops the horns over the eyes are large and the nasal horn small. In Monoclonius the nasal horn is large and those over the eyes are rudimentary.

The great variety of species that has been found in recent years shows that these Horned Dinosaurs were a numerous and varied race of which as yet we know only a few. Of their evolution we have little direct knowledge, but probably they are descended from the Iguanodonts and Camptosaurs of the Comanchic, and their quadrupedal gait, huge heads, short tails and other peculiarities are secondary specializations, their ancestors being bipedal, long-tailed, small headed and hornless.

The fine skulls of Triceratops, Monoclonius, Ceratops and Anchiceratops in the Museum collections illustrate the variety of these remarkable animals. Complete skeletons of the first two genera are being prepared for mounting and exhibition.

CHAPTER X.

GEOGRAPHICAL DISTRIBUTION OF DINOSAURS.

Remains of Dinosaurs have been found in all the continents, but chiefly in Europe and North America. Explorations in other parts of the world have not as yet been sufficient to show whether or not each continent developed especial kinds peculiar to it, nor to afford any reliable evidence as to whether the relations of the continents were different during the Mesozoic. Thus far, the Carnivorous group seems most widespread, for it alone has been found in Australia. The Sauropods or Amphibious Dinosaurs have been found in Europe, North America, India, Madagascar, Patagonia, and Africa, sufficient to show that their distribution was world wide with the possible exception of Australia, and probable exception of most oceanic islands (few of the modern oceanic islands existed at that time although there may well have been many others no longer extant). The Beaked Dinosaurs are more limited in their distribution, for none of them so far as at present known reached Australia or South America. But in the present stage of discovery it would be rash to conclude that they were surely limited to the regions where they have been discovered. It is not wholly clear as yet whether the Dinosaurian fauna that flourished at the end of the Jurassic in the north survived to the Upper Cretacic in the southern continents, but present evidence points that way, and indicates that the girdle of ocean which during the Cretacic depression encircled the northern world, formed a barrier which the Cretacic dinosaurian fauna never succeeded in crossing.

The earlier groups of Beaked Dinosaurs are found in both Europe and America, and in the Cretacic the Duck-billed and Armored groups are represented in both regions. The Horned Dinosaurs, however, are known with certainty only from North America.

While most of the important fossil specimens in this country have been found in the West, more fragmentary remains have been found on the Atlantic sea-board, and it is probable that they ranged all over the intervening region, wherever they found an environment suited to their particular needs.

CHAPTER XI.

COLLECTING DINOSAURS.

HOW AND WHERE THEY ARE FOUND.

The visitor who is introduced to the dinosaurs through the medium of books and pictures or of the skeletons exhibited in the great museums, finds it hard--well nigh impossible--to realize their existence. However willing he may be to accept on faith the reconstructions of the skeletons, the restorations of the animals and their supposed environment, it yet remains to him somewhat of a fairy-tale, a fanciful imaginative world peopled with ogres and dragons and belonging to the unreal "once upon a time" which has no connection with the ever present workaday world in which we live. Birds and squirrels, rabbits and foxes belong to this real world because he has seen them in his walks through the woods; even elephants and rhinoceroses, though his acquaintance be limited to menagerie specimens, seem fairly real--although one recalls the farmer's comment on first seeing a giraffe in the Zoological park: "There aint no sich animal." But dinosaurs--one easily realizes the state of mind that prompts the inquiry so often made by visitors to the Dinosaur Hall:--"they make these out of plaster, don't they?" So far as is consistent with good taste, the aim of the American Museum has been to enable the visitor to see for himself how much of plaster reconstruction there is to each skeleton, and to explain in the labels what the basis was for the reconstructed parts.

How They are Found. But to the collector these extinct animals are real enough. As he journeys over the western plains he sees the various living inhabitants thereof, birds and beasts, as well as men, pursuing their various modes of life; here and there he comes across the scattered skeletons or bones of modern animals lying strewn upon the surface of the ground or half buried in the soil of a cut bank. In the shales or sandstones that underlie the soil he finds the objects of his search, skeletons or bones of extinct animals, similarly disposed, but buried in rock instead of soft soil, and exposed in canyons and gullies cut through the solid rock. Each rock formation, he knows by precept and experience, carries its own peculiar fauna, its animals are different from those of the formation above and from those in the formation below. Days and weeks he may spend in fruitless search following along the outcrop of the formation, through rugged badlands, along steep canyon walls, around isolated points or buttes, without finding more than a few fragments, but spurred on by vivid interest and the rainbow prospect of some new or rare find. Finally perhaps, after innumerable disappointments, a trail of fragments leads up to a really promising prospect. A cautious investigation indicates that an articulated skeleton is buried at this point, and that not too much of it has "gone out" and rolled in weathered fragments down the slope. For the tedious and delicate process of disinterring the skeleton from the rock he will need to keep ever in mind the form and relations of each bone, the picture of the skeleton as it may have been when buried. The heavy ledges above are removed with pick and shovel, often with help of dynamite and a team and scraper. As he gets nearer to the stratum in which the bones lie the work must be more and more careful. A false blow with pick or chisel might destroy irreparably some important bony structure. Bit by bit he traces out the position and lay of the bones, working now mostly with awl and whisk-broom, uncovering the more massive portions, blocking out the delicate bones in the rock, soaking the exposed surfaces repeatedly with thin "gum" (mucilage) or shellac, channeling around and between the bones until they stand out on little pedestals above the quarry floor. Then, after the gum or shellac has dried thoroughly and hardened the soft parts, and the surfaces of bone exposed are further protected by pasting on a layer of tissue paper, it is ready for the "plaster jacket." This consists of strips of burlap dipped in plaster-of-paris and pasted over the surface of each block until top and sides, all but the pedestal on which it rests, are completely cased in, the strips being pressed and kneaded close to the surface of the block as they are laid on. When this jacket sets and dries the block is rigid and stiff enough to lift and turn over; the remains of the pedestal are trimmed off and the under surface is plastered like the rest. With large blocks it is often necessary to paste into the jacket, on upper or both sides, boards, scantling or sticks of wood to secure additional rigidity. For should the block "rack," or become shattered inside, even though no fragments were lost, the specimen would be more or less completely ruined.

The next stage will be packing in boxes with straw, hay or other materials, hauling to the railway and shipment to New York.

Arrived at the Museum, the boxes are unpacked, each block laid out on a table, the upper side of its plaster jacket softened with water and cut away, and the preparation of the bone begins. Always it is more or less cracked and broken up, but the fragments lie in their natural relations. Each piece must be lifted out, thoroughly cleaned from rock and dirt, and the fractured surfaces cemented together again. Parts of bones, especially the interior, are often rotted into dust while the harder outer surface is still preserved. The dust must be scraped out, the interior filled with a plaster cement, and the surface pieces re-set in position. Very often a steel rod is set into the plaster filling the interior of a bone, to secure additional strength.

After this preparation is completed, each part being soaked repeatedly with shellac until it will absorb no more, the bones can be handled and laid out for study or exhibition. Then, if they are to be mounted for a fossil skeleton, comes the work of restoring the missing parts. For this a plaster composition is used.

Where only parts of one side are missing the corresponding parts of the other side are used for model; where both sides are missing, other individuals or nearly related species may serve as a guide. But it is seldom wise to attempt restoration of a skeleton unless at least two-thirds of it is present; composite skeletons made up of the remains of several or many individuals, have been attempted, but they are dangerous experiments in animals so imperfectly known as are most of the dinosaurs. There is too much risk of including bones that pertain to other species or genera, and of introducing thereby into the restoration a more or less erroneous concept of the animal which it represents. The same criticism applies to an overly large amount of plaster restoration.

In some instances the missing parts of a skeleton are not restored, because, even though but a small part be gone, we have no good evidence to guide in its reconstruction. This gives an imperfect and sometimes misleading concept of what the whole skeleton was like, but it is better than restoring it erroneously. Usually with the more imperfect skeletons, a skull, a limb or some other characteristic parts may be placed on exhibition but the remainder of the specimen is stored in the study collections.

Where They are Found. The chief dinosaur localities in this country are along the flanks of the Rocky Mountains and the plains to the eastward, from Canada to Texas. Not that dinosaurs were any more abundant there than elsewhere. They probably ranged all over North America, and different kinds inhabited other continents as well. But in the East and the Middle West, the conditions were not favorable for preserving their remains, except in a few localities. Formations of this age are less extensive, especially those of the delta and coast-swamps which the dinosaurs frequented. And where they do occur, they are largely covered by vegetation and cannot be explored to advantage. In the arid Western regions these formations girdle the Rockies and outlying mountain chains for two-thousand miles from north to south, and are extensively exposed in great escarpments, river canyons and "badland" areas, bare of soil and vegetation and affording an immense stretch of exposed rock for the explorer. Much of this area indeed is desert, too far away from water to be profitably searched under present conditions, or too far away from railroads to allow of transportation of the finds at a reasonable expense. Fossils are much more common in certain parts of the region, and these localities have mostly been explored more or less thoroughly. But the field is far from being exhausted. New localities have been found and old localities re-explored in recent years, yielding specimens equal to or better than any heretofore discovered. And as the railroad and the automobile render new regions accessible, and the erosion of the formations by wind and rain brings new specimens to the surface, we may look forward to new discoveries for many years to come.

In other continents, except in Europe, there has been but little exploration for dinosaurs. Enough is known to assure us that they will yield faun?no less extensive and remarkable than our own. We are in fact only beginning to appreciate the vast extent and variety of these records of a past world.

In a preceding chapter it was shown that the chief formations in which dinosaur remains have been found belong to the end of the Jurassic and the end of the Cretacic periods. The Jurassic dinosaur formations skirt the Rockies and outlying mountain ranges but are often turned up on edge and poorly exposed, or barren of fossils. The richest collecting ground is in the Laramie Plains, between the Rockies and the Laramie range in south-central Wyoming, but important finds have also been made in Colorado and Utah. The Cretaceous Dinosaur formations extend somewhat further out on the plains to the eastward, and the best collecting regions thus far explored are in eastern Wyoming, central Montana and in Alberta, Canada.

THE FIRST DISCOVERY OF DINOSAURS IN THE WEST.

By Prof. S.W. Williston.

Most great discoveries are due rather to a state of mind, if I may use such an expression, than to accident. The discovery of the immense dinosaur deposits in the Rocky Mountains in March, 1877, may truthfully be called great, for nothing in paleontology has equalled it, and that it was made by three observers simultaneously can not be called purely an accident. These discoverers were Mr. O. Lucas, then a school teacher, later clergyman; Professor Arthur Lakes, then a teacher in the School of Mines at Golden, Colorado; and Mr. William Reed, then a section foreman of the Union Pacific Railroad at Como, Wyoming, later the curator of paleontology of the University of Wyoming--even as I write this, comes the notice of his death,-- the last. I knew them all, and the last two were long intimate friends.

In the autumn of 1878 I wrote the following:[19]

"The history of their discovery (the dinosaurs) is both interesting and remarkable. For years the beds containing them had been studied by geologists of experience, under the surveys of Hayden and King, but, with the possible exception of the half of a caudal vertebra, obtained by Hayden and described by Leidy as a species of Poikilopleuron, not a single fragment had been recognized. This is all the more remarkable from the fact that in several of the localities I have observed acres literally strewn with fragments of bones, many of them extremely characteristic and so large as to have taxed the strength of a strong man to lift them. Three of the localities known to me are in the immediate vicinity, if not upon the actual townsites of thriving villages, and for years numerous fragments have been collected by (or for) tourists and exhibited as fossil wood. The quantities hitherto obtained, though apparently so vast, are wholly unimportant in comparison with those awaiting the researches of geologists throughout the Rocky Mountain region. I doubt not that many hundreds of tons will eventually be exhumed." Rather a startling prophecy to make within eighteen months of their discovery, but it was hardly exaggerated.

It is impossible to say which of these three observers actually made the first discovery of Jurassic dinosaurs; whatever doubt there is is in favor of Mr. Reed.

Professor Lakes, accompanied by his friend Mr. E.L. Beckwith, an engineer, was, one day in March, 1877, hunting along the "hogback" in the vicinity of Morrison, Colorado, for fossil leaves in the Dakota Cretaceous sandstone which caps the ridge, when he saw a large block of sandstone with an enormous vertebra partly imbedded in it. He discussed the nature of the fossil with his friend (so he told me) and finally concluded that it was a fossil bone. He had recently come from England and had heard of Professor Phillips' discoveries of similar dinosaurs there. He knew of Professor Marsh of Yale from his recent discoveries of toothed birds in the chalk of Kansas, and reported the find to him. As a result, the specimen, rock and all, was shipped to him by express at ten cents a pound! And Professor Marsh immediately announced the discovery of Titanosaurus (Atlantosaurus) immanis, a huge dinosaur having a probable length of one hundred and fifteen feet and unknown height. And Professor Lakes was immediately set at work in the "Morrison quarry" near by, whence comes the accepted name of these dinosaur beds in the Rocky Mountains. Professor Lakes once showed me the exact spot where he found his first specimen.

Mr. Lucas, teaching his first term of a country school that spring in Garden Park near Canyon City, as an amateur botanist was interested in the plants of the vicinity. Rambling through the adjacent hills in search of them, in March, 1877, he stumbled upon some fragments of fossil bones in a little ravine not far from the famous quarry later worked for Professor Marsh. He recognized them as fossils and they greatly excited, not only his curiosity, but the curiosity of the neighbors. He had heard of the late Professor Cope and sent some of the bones to him, who promptly labelled them Camarasaurus supremus.

The announcement of these discoveries promptly brought Mr. David Baldwin, Professor Marsh's collector in New Mexico, to the scene. Only a few months previously he had discovered fossil bones in the red beds of New Mexico, the since famous Permian deposits. He naturally explored the same beds at Canyon City, immediately below the dinosaur deposits, and soon found the still very problematical Hallopus skeleton, at their very top, a specimen which after nearly forty years remains unique of its kind.

A few years earlier Professor Marsh, on his way east from the Tertiary deposits of western Wyoming, had stopped at Como, Wyoming, to observe the strange salamanders, or "fish with legs" as they were widely known, so abundant in the lake at that place, about whose transformations he later wrote a paper, perhaps the only one on modern vertebrates that he ever published. While he was there Mr. Carlin, the station agent, showed him some fossil bone fragments, so Mr. Reed told me, that they had picked up in the vicinity, and about which Professor Marsh made some comments. But he was so engrossed with the other discoveries he was then making that he did not follow up the suggestion. Had he done so the discovery of the "Jurassic Dinosaurs" would have been made five years earlier.

Mr. Reed, tramping over the famous Como hills after game--he had been a professional hunter of game for the construction camps of the Union Pacific Railroad--in the winter and spring of 1877, observed some fossil bones just south of the railway station that excited his curiosity. But he and Mr. Carlin did not make their discovery known to Professor Marsh till the following autumn, and then under assumed names, fearing that they would be robbed of their discovery. I was sent to Como in November of 1877 from Canyon City. I got off the train at the station after midnight, and enquired for the nearest hotel--(the station comprised two houses only), and where I could find Messrs. Smith and Robinson. I was told that the section house was the only hotel in the place and that these gentlemen lived in the country and that there was no regular bus-line yet running to their ranch. A freshly opened box of cigars, however, helped clear up things, and I joined Mr. Reed the next day in opening "Quarry No. 1" of the Como hills. Inasmuch as the mercury in the thermometer during the next two months seldom reached zero--upward I mean--the opening of this famous deposit was made under difficulties. That so much "head cheese," as we called it, was shipped to Professor Marsh was more the fault of the weather and his importunities than our carelessness. However, we found some of the types of dinosaurs that have since become famous.

I joined Professor Lakes at the Morrison quarry in early September of 1877, and helped dig out some of the bones of Atlantosaurus. A few weeks later I was sent to Canyon City to help Professor Mudge, my old teacher, and Mr. Felch, who had begun work there in the famous "Marsh Quarry". It was here that we found the type of Diplodocus.

The hind leg, pelvis and much of the tail of this specimen lay in very orderly arrangement in the sandstone near the edge of the quarry, but the bones were broken into innumerable pieces. After consultation we decided that they were too much broken to be worth saving--and so most of them went over into the dump. Sacrilege, doubtless, the modern collector will say, but we did not know much about the modern methods of collecting in those days, and moreover we were in too much of a hurry to get the new discoveries to Yale College to take much pains with them. I did observe that the caudal vertebrae had very peculiar chevrons, unlike others that I had seen, and so I attempted to save some samples of them by pasting them up with thick layers of paper. Had we only known of plaster-of-paris and burlap the whole specimen might easily have been saved. Later, when I reached New Haven, I took off the paper and called Professor Marsh's attention to the strange chevrons. And Diplodocus was the result.

My own connection with the discoveries of these old dinosaurs continued only through the following summer, in Wyoming, when we added the first mammals from the hills immediately back of the station, and the types of some of the smaller dinosaurs, and when we explored the vicinity for other deposits, on Rock Creek and in the Freeze Out Mountains.

How many tons of these fossils have since been dug up from these deposits in the Rocky Mountains is beyond computation. My prophecy of hundreds of tons has been fulfilled; and they are preserved in many museums of the world.

S.W. WILLISTON.

THE DINOSAURS OF THE BONE-CABIN QUARRY.[20]

By Henry Fairfield Osborn.

One is often asked the questions: "How do you find fossils?" "How do you know where to look for them?" One of the charms of the fossil-hunter's life is the variety, the element of certainty combined with the gambling element of chance. Like the prospector for gold, the fossil-hunter may pass suddenly from the extreme of dejection to the extreme of elation. Luck comes in a great variety of ways: sometimes as the result of prolonged and deliberate scientific search in a region which is known to be fossiliferous; sometimes in such a prosaic manner as the digging of a well. Among discoveries of a highly suggestive, almost romantic kind, perhaps none is more remarkable than the one I shall now describe.

Discovery of the Great Dinosaur Quarry. In central Wyoming, at the head of a "draw," or small valley, not far from the Medicine Bow River, lies the ruin of a small and unique building, which marks the site of the greatest "find" of extinct animals made in a single locality in any part of the world. The fortunate fossil-hunter who stumbled on this site was Mr. Walter Granger of the American Museum expedition of 1897.

In the spring of 1898, as I approached the hillock on which the ruin stands, I observed, among the beautiful flowers, the blooming cacti, and the dwarf bushes of the desert, what were apparently numbers of dark-brown boulders. On closer examination, it proved that there is really not a single rock, hardly even a pebble, on this hillock; all these apparent boulders are ponderous fossils which have slowly accumulated or washed out on the surface from a great dinosaur bed beneath. A Mexican sheep-herder had collected some of these petrified bones for the foundations of his cabin, the first ever built of such strange materials. The excavation of a promising outcrop was almost immediately rewarded by finding a thigh-bone nearly six feet in length which sloped downward into the earth, running into the lower leg and finally into the foot, with all the respective parts lying in the natural position as in life. This proved to be the previously unknown hind limb of the great dinosaur Diplodocus.

In this manner the "Bone-Cabin Quarry" was discovered and christened. The total contents of the quarry are represented in the diagram (not reprinted.) It has given us, by dint of six successive years of hard work, the materials for an almost complete revival of the life of the Laramie region as it was in the days of the dinosaurs. By the aid of workmen of every degree of skill, by grace of the accumulated wisdom of the nineteenth century, by the constructive imagination, by the aid of the sculptor and the artist, we can summon these living forms and the living environment from the vasty deep of the past.

The Famous Como Bluffs. The circumstances leading up to our discovery serve to introduce the story. From 1890 to 1897 we had been steadily delving into the history of the Age of Mammals, in deposits dating from two hundred thousand to three million years back, as we rudely estimate geological time. In the course of seven years such substantial progress had been made that I decided to push into the history of the Age of Reptiles also, and, following the pioneers, Marsh and Cope, to begin exploration in the period which at once marks the dawn of mammalian life and the climax of the evolution of the great amphibious dinosaurs.

In the spring of 1897 we accordingly began exploration in the heart of the Laramie Plains, on the Como Bluffs. On arrival, we found numbers of massive bones strewn along the base of these bluffs, tumbled from their stratum above, too weather-worn to attract collectors, and serving only to remind one of the time when these animals--the greatest, by far, that nature has ever produced on land--were monarchs of the world.

Aroused from sleep on a clear evening in camp by the heavy rumble of a passing Union Pacific freight-train[21], I shall never forget my meditations on the contrast between the imaginary picture of the great Age of Dinosaurs, fertile in cycads and in a wonderful variety of reptiles, and the present age of steam, of heavy locomotives toiling through the semi-arid and partly desert Laramie Plains.

So many animals had already been removed from these bluffs that we were not very sanguine of finding more; but after a fortnight our prospecting was rewarded by finding parts of skeletons of the long-limbed dinosaur Diplodocus and of the heavy-limbed dinosaur Brontosaurus. The whole summer was occupied in taking these animals out for shipment to the East, the so-called "plaster method" of removal being applied with the greatest success. Briefly, this is a surgical device applied on a large scale for the "setting" of the much-fractured bones of a fossilized skeleton. It consists in setting great blocks of the skeleton, stone and all, in a firm capsule of plaster subsequently reinforced by great splints of wood, firmly drawn together with wet rawhide. The object is to keep all the fragments and splinters of bone together until it can reach the skilful hands of the museum preparator.

The Rock Waves Connecting the Bluffs and the Quarry. The Como Bluffs are about ten miles south of the Bone-Cabin Quarry; between them is a broad stretch of the Laramie Plains. The exposed bone layer in the two localities is of the same age, and originally was a continuous level stratum which may be designated as the "dinosaur beds;" but this stratum, disturbed and crowded by the uplifting of the not far-distant Laramie range of mountains and the Freeze Out Hills, was thrown into a number of great folds or rock waves. Large portions, especially of the upfolds, or "anticlines," of the waves, have been subsequently removed by erosion; the edges of these upfolds have been exposed, thus weathering out their fossilized contents, while downfolds are still buried beneath the earth for the explorers of coming centuries.

Therefore, as one rides across the country to-day from the bluffs to the quarry, startling the intensely modern fauna, the prong-horn antelopes, jack-rabbits, and sage-chickens, he is passing over a vast graveyard which has been profoundly folded and otherwise shaken up and disturbed. Sometimes one finds the bone layer removed entirely, sometimes horizontal, sometimes oblique, and again dipping directly into the heart of the earth. This layer (dinosaur beds) is not more than two hundred and seventy-four feet in thickness, and is altogether of fresh-water origin; but as a proof of the oscillations of the earth-level both before and after this great thin sheet of fresh-water rock was so widely spread, there are evidences of the previous invasion of the sea (ichthyosaur beds) and of the subsequent invasion of the sea (mosasaur beds) in the whole Rocky Mountain region.

In traveling through the West, when once one has grasped the idea of continental oscillation, or submergence and emergence of the land, of the sequence of the marine and fresh-water deposits in laying down these pages of earth-history, he will know exactly where to look for this wonderful layer-bed of the giant dinosaurs; he will find that, owing to the uplift of various mountain-ranges, it outcrops along the entire eastern face of the Rockies, around the Black Hills, and in all parts of the Laramie Plains; it yields dinosaur bones everywhere, but by no means so profusely or so perfectly as in the two famous localities we are describing.

How the Skeletons Lie in the Bluffs and Quarry. At the bluffs single animals lie from twenty to one hundred feet apart; one rarely finds a whole skeleton, such as that of Marsh's Brontosaurus excelsus, the finest specimen ever secured here, which is now one of the treasures of the Yale museum. More frequently a half or a third of a skeleton lies together.

In the Bone-Cabin Quarry, on the other hand, we came across a veritable Noah's-ark deposit, a perfect museum of all the animals of the period. Here are the largest of the giant dinosaurs closely mingled with the remains of the smaller but powerful carnivorous dinosaurs which preyed upon them, also those of the slow and heavy-moving armored dinosaurs of the period, as well as of the lightest and most bird-like of the dinosaurs. Finely rounded, complete limbs from eight to ten feet in length are found, especially those of the carnivorous dinosaurs, perfect even to the sharply pointed and recurved tips of their toes. Other limbs and bones are so crushed and distorted by pressure that it is not worth while removing them. Sixteen series of vertebrae were found strung together; among these were eight long strings of tail-bones. The occurrence of these tails is less surprising when we come to study the important and varied functions of the tail in these animals, and the consequent connection of the tail-bones by means of stout tendons and ligaments which held them together for a long period after death. Skulls are fragile and rare in the quarry, because in every one of these big skeletons there were no fewer than ninety distinct bones which exceeded the head in size, the excess in most cases being enormous.

[Illustration: Fig. 45.--COLLECTING DINOSAURS AT BONE-CABIN QUARRY. a. The overlying soil and rocks are loosened with a pick and removed with team and scraper down to the fossil layer.

b. The fossil layer is carefully prospected with small tools, chisels, awls and whisk brooms exposing the bones as they lie in the rocks.

c. The blocks containing the fossils are channelled around, plastered over top and sides, undercut and carefully turned over and the under side trimmed and plastered.

d. The blocks are then packed in boxes or crates with hay or any other available packing material.

e. Boxes are loaded on wagons and hauled across country to the railroad.

f. Boxes are finally loaded on cars and shipped through to New York City.]

The bluffs appear to represent the region of an ancient shoreline, such conditions as we have depicted in the restoration of Brontosaurus (fig. 22)-- the sloping banks of a muddy estuary or of a lagoon, either bare tidal flats or covered with vegetation. Evidently the dinosaurs were buried at or near the spot where they perished.

The Bone-Cabin Quarry deposit represents entirely different conditions. The theory that it is the accumulation of a flood is, in my opinion, improbable, because a flood would tend to bring entire skeletons down together, distribute them widely, and bury them rapidly. A more likely theory is that this was the area of an old river-bar, which in its shallow waters arrested the more or less decomposed and scattered carcasses which had slowly drifted down-stream toward it, including a great variety of dinosaurs, crocodiles, and turtles, collected from many points up-stream. Thus were brought together the animals of a whole region, a fact which vastly enhances the interest of this deposit.

The Giant Herbivorous Dinosaurs. By far the most imposing of these animals are those which may be popularly designated as the great or giant dinosaurs. The name, derived from deinos terrible, and sauros lizard, refers to the fact that they appeared externally like enormous lizards, with very long limbs, necks, and tails. They were actually remotely related to the tuatera lizard of New Zealand, and still more remotely to the true lizards.

No land animals have ever approached these giant dinosaurs in size, and naturally the first point of interest is the architecture of the skeleton. The backbone is indeed a marvel. The fitness of the construction consists, like that of the American truss-bridge, in attaining the maximum of strength with the minimum of weight. It is brought about by dispensing with every cubic millimeter of bone which can be spared without weakening the vertebrae for the various stresses and strains to which they were subjected, and these must have been tremendous in an animal from sixty to seventy feet in length. The bodies of the vertebrae are of hour-glass shape, with great lateral and interior cavities; the arches are constructed on the T-iron principle of the modern bridge-builder, the back spines are tubular, the interior is spongy, these devices being employed in great variety, and constituting a mechanical triumph of size, lightness, and strength combined. Comparing a great chambered dinosaurian (Camarasaurus) vertebra (see above) with the weight per cubic inch of an ostrich vertebra, we reach the astonishing conclusion that it weighed only twenty-one pounds, or half the weight of a whale vertebra of the same bulk. The skeleton of a whale seventy-four feet in length has recently been found by Mr. F.A. Lucas of the Brooklyn Museum to weigh seventeen thousand nine hundred and twenty pounds. The skeleton of a dinosaur of the same length may be roughly estimated as not exceeding ten thousand pounds.

Proofs of Rapid Movements on Land. Lightness of skeleton is a walking or running or flying adaptation, and not at all a swimming one; a swimming animal needs gravity in its skeleton, because sufficient buoyancy in the water is always afforded by the lungs and soft tissues of the body. The extraordinary lightness of these dinosaur vertebrae may therefore be put forward as proof of supreme fitness for the propulsion of an enormous frame during occasional incursions upon land[22]. There are additional facts which point to land progression, such as the point in the tail where the flexible structure suddenly becomes rigid, as shown in the diagram of vertebrae below; the component joints are so solid and flattened on the lower surface that they seem to demonstrate fitness to support partly the body in a tripodal position like that of a kangaroo. I have therefore hazarded the view that even some of these enormous dinosaurs were capable of raising themselves on their hind limbs, lightly resting on the middle portion of the tail. In such a position the animal would have been capable not only of browsing among the higher branches of trees, but of defending itself against the carnivorous dinosaurs by using its relatively short but heavy front limbs to ward off attacks.

There are also indications of aquatic habits in some of the giant dinosaurs which render it probable that a considerable part of their life was led in the water. One of these indications is the backward position of the nostrils. Many, but not all, water-living mammals and reptiles have the nostrils on top of the head, in order to breathe more readily when the head is partly immersed. Another fact of note, although perhaps less conclusive, is the fitness of the tail for use while moving about in the water, if not in rapid swimming.

The great tail, measuring from twenty-eight to thirty feet, was one of the most remarkable structures in these animals, and undoubtedly served a great variety of purposes, propelling while in the water, balancing and supporting and defending while on land. In Diplodocus it was most perfectly developed from its muscular base to its delicate and whip-like tip, perhaps for all these functions.

The Three Kinds of Giant Dinosaurs. It is very remarkable that three distinct kinds of these great dinosaurs lived at the same time in the same general region, as proved by the fact that their remains are freely commingled in the quarry.

What were the differences in food and habits, in structure and in gait, which prevented that direct and active competition between like types in the struggle for existence which in the course of nature always leads to the extermination of one or the other type? In the last three years we have discovered very considerable differences of structure which make it appear that these animals, while of the same or nearly the same linear dimensions, did not enter into direct competition either for food or for territory.

The dinosaur named Diplodocus by Marsh is the most completely known of the three. Our very first discovery in the Bone-Cabin Quarry gave us the hint that Diplodocus was distinguished by relatively long, slender limbs, and that it may be popularly known as the "long-limbed dinosaur." The great skeleton found in the Como Bluffs enabled me to restore for the first time the posterior half of one of these animals estimated as sixty feet in length, the hips and tail especially being in a perfect state of preservation. A larger animal, nearer seventy feet in length, including the anterior half of the body, and still more complete, was discovered about ten miles north of the quarry, and is now in the Carnegie Museum in Pittsburg. Combined, these two animals have furnished a complete knowledge of the great bony frame. The head is only two feet long, and is, therefore, small out of all proportion to the great body. The neck measures twenty-one feet four inches, and is by far the longest and largest neck known in any animal living or extinct. The back is relatively very short, measuring ten feet eight inches. The vertebr?of the hip measure two feet and three inches. The tail measures from thirty-two to forty feet. We thus obtain, as a moderate estimate of the total length of the animal, sixty-eight to seventy feet. The restored skeleton, published by Mr. J.B. Hatcher in July, 1901, and partly embodying our results, gave to science the first really accurate knowledge of the length of these animals, which hitherto had been greatly overestimated. The highest point in the body was above the hips; here in fact, was the center of power and motion, because, as observed above, the tail fairly balanced the anterior part of the body.

The restoration by Mr. Knight is drawn from a very careful model made under my direction, in which the proportions of the animal are precisely estimated. It is, I think, accurate--for a restoration--as well as interesting and up-to-date. These restorations are the "working hypotheses" of our science; they express the present state of our knowledge, and, being subject to modification by future discoveries, are liable to constant change.

By contrast, the second type of giant dinosaur, the Brontosaurus, or "thunder saurian" of Marsh, as shown in the restoration (fig. 22), was far more massive in structure and relatively shorter in body. Five more or less complete skeletons are now to be seen in the Yale, American, Carnegie, and Field Columbian museums. In 1898 we discovered in the bluffs, about three miles west of the Bone-Cabin Quarry, the largest of these animals which has yet been found; it was worked out with great care and is now being restored and mounted complete in the American Museum. The thigh-bone is enormous, measuring five feet eight inches in length, and is relatively of greater mass than that of Diplodocus. The neck, chest, hips, and tail are correspondingly massive. The neck is relatively shorter, however, measuring eighteen feet, while in Diplodocus it measures over twenty-one feet. The total length of this massive specimen is estimated at sixty-three feet, or from six to eight feet less than the largest "long-limbed" dinosaur. The height of the skeleton at the hips is fifteen feet. There is less direct evidence that the "thunder saurian" had the power of raising its fore quarters in the air than in the case of the "light-limbed saurian," because no bend or supporting point in the tail has been distinctly observed.

The third type of giant dinosaur is the less completely known "chambered saurian," the Camarasaurus of Cope or Morosaurus of Marsh, an animal more quadrupedal in gait or walking more habitually on all fours, like the great Cetiosaurus, or "whale saurian," discovered near Oxford, England. With its shorter tail and heavier fore limbs, it is still less probable that this animal had the power of raising the anterior part of its body from the ground. Of a related type, perhaps, is the largest dinosaur ever found; this is the Brachiosaurus, limb-bones of which were discovered in central Colorado in 1901 and are now preserved in the Field Columbian Museum of Chicago. Its thigh-bone is six feet eight inches in length, and its upper arm-bone, or humerus, is even slightly longer.

Feeding Habits of the Giant Dinosaurs. We still have to solve one of the most perplexing problems of fossil physiology; how did the very small head, provided with light jaws, slender and spoon-shaped teeth confined to the anterior region, suffice to provide food for these monsters? I have advanced the idea that the food of Diplodocus consisted of some very abundant and nutritious species of water-plant; that the clawed feet were used in uprooting such plants, while the delicate anterior teeth were employed only for drawing them out of the water; that the plants were drawn down the throat in large quantities without mastication, since there were no grinding or back teeth whatever in this animal. Unfortunately for this theory, it is now found that the front feet were not provided with many claws, there being only a single claw on the inner side. Nevertheless by some such means as this, these enormous animals could have obtained sufficient food in the water to support their great bulk.

The Carnivorous Dinosaurs. Mingling with the larger bones in the quarry are the more or less perfect remains of swamp turtles, of dwarf crocodiles, of the entirely different group of plated dinosaurs, or Stegosauria, but especially of two entirely distinct kinds of large and small flesh-eating dinosaurs. The latter rounded out and gave variety to the dinosaur society, and there is no doubt that they served the savage but useful purpose, rendered familiar by the doctrine of Malthus, of checking overpopulation. These fierce animals had the same remote ancestry as the giant dinosaurs, but had gradually acquired entirely different habits and appearance.

Far inferior in size, they were superior in agility, exclusively bipedal, with very long, powerful hind limbs, upon which they advanced by running or springing, and with short fore limbs, the exact uses of which are difficult to ascertain. Both hands and feet were provided with powerful tearing claws. On the hind foot is the back claw, so characteristic of the birds, which during the Triassic period left its faint impression almost everywhere in the famous Connecticut valley imprints of these animals. That the fore limb and hand were of some distinct use is proved by the enormous size of the thumb-claw; while the hand may not have conveyed food to the mouth, it may have served to seize and tear the prey. As to the actual pose in feeding, there can be little doubt as to its general similarity to that of the Raptores among the birds, as suggested to me by Dr. Wortman (see fig. 10); one of the hind feet rested on the prey, the other upon the ground, the body being further balanced or supported by the vertebr?of the tail. The animal was thus in a position to apply its teeth and exert all the power of its very powerful arched back in tearing off its food. That the gristle of the bone or cartilage was very palatable is attested not only by the toothmarks upon these bones, but by many similar markings found in the Bone-Cabin Quarry.

The Bird-Catching Dinosaur. Of all the bird-like dinosaurs which have been discovered, none possesses greater similitude to the birds than the gem of the quarry, the little animal about seven feet in length which we have named Ornitholestes, or the "bird-catching dinosaur." It was a marvel of speed, agility, and delicacy of construction. Externally its bones are simple and solid-looking, but as a matter of fact they are mere shells, the walls being hardly thicker than paper, the entire interior of the bone having been removed by the action of the same marvelous law of adaptation which sculptured the vertebr?of its huge contemporaries. There is no evidence, however, that these hollow bones were filled with air from the lungs, as in the case of the bones of birds. The foot is bird-like; the hand is still more so; in fact, no dinosaur hand has ever before been found which so closely mimics that of a bird in the great elongation of the first or index-finger, in the abbreviation of the thumb and middle finger, and in the reduction of the ring-finger. These fingers, with sharp claws, were not strong enough for climbing, and the only special fitness we have been able to imagine is that they were used for the grasping of a light and agile prey (see figs. 17, 18.)

Another reason for the venture of designating this animal as the "bird-catcher" is that the Jurassic birds (not thus far discovered in America, but known from the Archaeopteryx of Germany) were not so active or such strong fliers as existing birds; in fact, they were not unlike the little dinosaur itself. They were toothed, long-tailed, short-armed, the body was feathered instead of scaled; they rose slowly from the ground. This renders it probable that they were the prey of the smaller pneumatic-built dinosaurs such as the present animal.

This hypothetical bird-catcher seems to have been designed to spring upon a delicately built prey, the structure being the very antipode of that of the large carnivorous dinosaurs. A difficulty in the bird-catching theory, namely, that the teeth are not as sharp as one would expect to find them in a flesh-eater, is somewhat offset by the similarity of the teeth to those of the bird-eating monitor lizards (Varanus), which are not especially sharp.

The Great Yield of the Quarry. Our explorations in the quarry began in the spring of 1898, and have continued ever since during favorable weather. The total area explored at the close of the sixth year was seven thousand two hundred and fifty square feet. Not one of the twelve-foot squares into which the quarry was plotted lacked its covering of bones, and in some cases the bones were two or three deep. Each year we have expected to come to the end of this great deposit, but it still yields a large return, although we have reason to believe that we have exhausted the richest portions.

We have taken up four hundred and eighty-three parts of animals, some of which may belong to the same individuals. These were packed in two hundred and seventy-five boxes, representing a gross weight of nearly one hundred thousand pounds. Reckoning from the number of thigh-bones, we reach, as a rough estimate of the total, seventy-three animals of the following kinds: giant herbivorous dinosaurs, 44; plated herbivorous dinosaurs, or stegosaurs, 3; iguanodonts or smaller herbivorous dinosaurs, 4; large carnivorous dinosaurs, 6; small carnivorous dinosaurs, 3; crocodiles, 4; turtles, 5. But this represents only a part of the whole deposit, which we know to be of twice the extent already explored, and these figures do not include the bones which were partly washed out and used in the construction of the Bone-Cabin. The grand total would probably include parts of over one hundred giant dinosaurs.

The Struggle for Existence Among the Dinosaurs. Never in the whole history of the world as we now know it have there been such remarkable land scenes as were presented when the reign of these titanic reptiles was at its climax. It was also the prevailing life-picture of England, Germany, South America, and India. We can imagine herds of these creatures from fifty to eighty feet in length, with limbs and gait analogous to those of gigantic elephants, but with bodies extending through the long, flexible, and tapering necks into the diminutive heads, and reaching back into the equally long and still more tapering tails. The four or five varieties which existed together were each fitted to some special mode of life; some living more exclusively on land, others for longer periods in the water.

The competition for existence was not only with the great carnivorous dinosaurs, but with other kinds of herbivorous dinosaurs (the iguanodonts), which had much smaller bodies to sustain and a much superior tooth mechanism for the taking of food.

The cutting off of this giant dinosaur dynasty was nearly if not quite simultaneous the world over. The explanation which is deducible from similar catastrophes to other large types of animals is that a very large frame, with a limited and specialized set of teeth fitted only to a certain special food, is a dangerous combination of characters. Such a monster organism is no longer adaptable; any serious change of conditions which would tend to eliminate the special food would also eliminate these great animals as a necessary consequence.

There is an entirely different class of explanations, however, to be considered, which are consistent both with the continued fitness of structure of the giant dinosaurs themselves and with the survival of their especial food; such, for example, as the introduction of a new enemy more deadly even than the great carnivorous dinosaurs. Among such theories the most ingenious is that of the late Professor Cope, who suggested that some of the small, inoffensive, and inconspicuous forms of Jurassic mammals, of the size of the shrew and the hedgehog, contracted the habit of seeking out the nests of these dinosaurs, gnawing through the shells of their eggs, and thus destroying the young. The appearance, or evolution, of any egg-destroying animals, whether reptiles or mammals, which could attack this great race at such a defenseless point would be rapidly followed by its extinction. We must accordingly be on the alert for all possible theories of extinction; and these theories themselves will fall under the universal principle of the survival of the fittest until we approximate or actually hit upon the truth.

FOSSIL HUNTING BY BOAT IN CANADA.

By Barnum Brown.

"How do you know where to look for fossils?" is a common question. In general it may be answered that the surface of North America has been pretty well explored by government surveys and scientific expeditions and the geologic age of the larger areas determined. Most important in determining the geologic sequence of the earth's strata are the fossil remains of animal and plant life. A grouping of distinct species of fossils correlated with stratigraphic characters in the rocks determines these subdivisions. When a collection of fossils is desired to represent a certain period, exploring parties are sent to these known areas. Sometimes however, chance information leads up to most important discoveries, such as resulted from the work of the past two seasons in Alberta, Canada.

A visitor to the Museum, Mr. J.L. Wagner, while examining our mineral collections saw the large bones in the Reptile Hall and remarked to the Curator of Mineralogy that he had seen many similar bones near his ranch in the Red Deer Canyon of Alberta. After talking some time an invitation was extended to the writer to visit his home and prospect the canyon. Accordingly in the fall of 1909 a preliminary trip was made to the locality.

From Didsbury, a little town north of Calgary, the writer drove eastward ninety miles to the Red Deer River through a portion of the newly opened grain belt of Alberta, destined in the near future to produce a large part of the world's bread. Near the railroad the land is mostly under cultivation and comfortable homes and bountiful grain fields testify to the rich nature of the soil. A few miles eastward the brushland gives way to a level expanse of grass-covered prairie dotted here and there by large and small lakes probably of glacial origin. Mile after mile the road follows section lines and one is rarely out of sight of the house of some "homesteader." It is through this level farm land that the Red Deer River wends its way flowing through a canyon far below the surface. Near Wagner's ranch the canyon was prospected and so many bones found that it appeared most desirable to do extended searching along the river.

Usually fossils are found in "bad lands," where extensive areas are denuded of grass and the surface eroded into hills and ravines. A camp is located near some spring or stream and collectors ride or walk over miles of these exposures in each direction till the region is thoroughly explored. Quite different are conditions on the Red Deer River. Cutting through the prairie land the river had formed a canyon two to five hundred feet deep and rarely more than a mile wide at the top. In places the walls are nearly perpendicular and the river winds in its narrow valley, touching one side then crossing to the other so that it is impossible to follow up or down its course any great distance even on horseback.

It was evident that the most feasible way to work these banks was from a boat; consequently in the summer of 1910 our party proceeded to the town of Red Deer, where the Calgary-Edmonton railroad crosses the river. There a flatboat, twelve by thirty feet in dimension, was constructed on lines similar to a western ferry boat, having a carrying capacity of eight tons with a twenty-two foot oar at each end to direct its course. The rapid current averaging about four miles per hour precluded any thought of going up stream in a large boat, so it was constructed on lines sufficiently generous to form a living boat as well as to carry the season's collection of fossils.

Supplied with a season's provisions, lumber for boxes, and plaster for encasing bones, we began our fossil cruise down a canyon which once echoed songs of the Bois brul? for this was at one time the fur territory of the great Hudson Bay Company.

No more interesting or instructive journey has ever been taken by the writer. High up on the plateau, buildings and haystacks proclaim a well-settled country, but habitations are rarely seen from the river and for miles we floated through picturesque solitude unbroken save by the roar of the rapids.

Especially characteristic of this canyon are the slides where the current setting against the bank has undermined it until a mountain of earth slips into the river, in some cases almost choking its course. A continual sorting thus goes on, the finer material being carried away while the boulders are left as barriers forming slow moving reaches of calm water and stretches of rapids difficult to navigate during low water. In one of these slides we found several small mammal jaws and teeth not known before from Canada, associated with fossil clam shells of Eocene age.

The long midsummer days in latitude 52?gave many working hours, but with frequent stops to prospect the banks we rarely floated more than twenty miles per day. An occasional flock of ducks and geese were disturbed as our boat approached and bank beaver houses were frequently passed, but few of the animals were seen during the daytime. Tying the boat to a tree at night we would go ashore to camp among the trees where after dinner pipes were smoked in the glow of a great camp fire. Only a fossil hunter or a desert traveler can fully appreciate the luxury of abundant wood and running water. In the stillness of the night the underworld was alive and many little feet rustled the leaves where daylight disclosed no sound. Then the beaver and muskrat swam up to investigate this new intruder, while from the tree-tops came the constant query, "Who! Who!"

For seventy miles the country is thickly wooded with pine and poplar, the stately spruce trees silhouetted against the sky adding a charm to the ever changing scene. Nature has also been kind to the treeless regions beyond, for underneath the fertile prairie, veins of good lignite coal of varying thickness are successively cut by the river. In many places these are worked in the river banks during winter. One vein of excellent quality is eighteen feet thick, although usually they are much thinner. The government right has been taken to mine most of this coal outcropping along the river.

Along the upper portion of the stream are banks of Eocene age, from which shells and mammal jaws were secured, but near the town of Content where the river bends southward, a new series of rocks appeared and in these our search was rewarded by finding dinosaur bones similar to those seen at Wagner's ranch. Specimens were found in increasing numbers as we continued our journey, and progress down the river was necessarily much slower. Frequently the boat would be tied up a week or more at one camp while we searched the banks, examining the cliffs layer by layer that no fossil might escape observation. With the little dingey the opposite side of the river was reached so that both sides were covered at the same time from one camp. As soon as a mile or more had been prospected or a new specimen secured, the boat was dropped down to a new convenient anchorage. Box after box was added to the collection till scarcely a cubit's space remained unoccupied on board our fossil ark.

Where prairie badlands are eroded in innumerable buttes and ravines it is always doubtful if one has seen all exposures, so there was peculiar satisfaction in making a thorough search of these river banks knowing that few if any fossils had escaped observation. On account of the heavy rainfall and frequent sliding of banks new fossils are exposed every season so that in a few years these same banks can again be explored profitably. This river will become as classic hunting ground for reptile remains as the Badlands of South Dakota are for mammals.

Although the summer days are long in this latitude the season is short and thousands of geese flying southward foretell the early winter. Where the temperature is not infrequently forty to sixty degrees below zero in winter, it is difficult to think of a time when a warm climate could have prevailed, yet such condition is indicated by the fossil plants.

When the weather became too cold to work with plaster, the fossils were shipped from a branch railroad forty-five miles distant, the camp material was stored for the winter and with block and tackle the big boat was hauled up on shore above the reach of high water.

In the summer of 1911 the boat was recalked and again launched when we continued our search from the point at which work closed the previous year. During the summer we were visited by the Museum's President, Prof. Henry Fairfield Osborn, and one of the Trustees, Mr. Madison Grant. A canoeing trip, one of great interest and pleasure, was taken with our visitors covering two hundred and fifty miles down the river from the town of Red Deer, during which valuable material was added to the collection and important geological data secured.

As a result of the Canadian work the Museum is enriched by a magnificent collection of Cretaceous fossils some of which are new to science.

FOOTNOTES:

[Footnote 19: Transactions Kansas Academy of Science, p. 43.]

[Footnote 20: From Fossil Wonders of the West. Century Magazine 1904, vol. lxviii, pp. 680-694. Reprinted by permission.]

[Footnote 21: At this time the Union Pacific Railroad directly passed the bluffs; in the recent improvement of the grade the main line has been moved to the south.--H.F.O.]

[Footnote 22: A different interpretation of this contraction is given upon p. 68.]